COOKING
Month by Month

TREASURE PRESS

COOKING
Month by Month

MARY NORWAK

The author and publishers would like to thank
The Boots Company for supplying a selection of their merchandise
for use in the photographs. Thanks also to
John Lewis for the patchwork quilt, page 57
Liberty and Co. Limited for the china, page 171
David Mellor for the preserving pan, page 29

Front cover photograph by Paul Kemp
Photography by Paul Williams
Home Economist Carol Bowen
Line illustrations by Meg Rutherford

First published in Great Britain
for general circulation in 1984 by
The Hamlyn Publishing Group Limited

This edition published in 1988 by
Treasure Press
59 Grosvenor Street
London W1

ISBN 1 85051 314 7

Printed in Hungary

Contents

Useful Facts and Figures

Notes on metrication

In this book quantities are given in metric and Imperial measures. Exact conversion from Imperial to metric measures does not usually give very convenient working quantities and so the metric measures have been rounded off into units of 25 grams. The table below shows the recommended equivalents.

Ounces	Approx g to nearest whole figure	Recommended conversion to nearest unit of 25
1	28	25
2	57	50
3	85	75
4	113	100
5	142	150
6	170	175
7	198	200
8	227	225
9	255	250
10	283	275
11	312	300
12	340	350
13	368	375
14	396	400
15	425	425
16 (1 lb)	454	450
17	482	475
18	510	500
19	539	550
20 (1¼ lb)	567	575

Note: *When converting quantities over 20 oz first add the appropriate figures in the centre column, then adjust to the nearest unit of 25. As a general guide, 1 kg (1000 g) equals 2·2 lb or about 2 lb 3 oz. This method of conversion gives good results in nearly all cases, although in certain pastry and cake recipes a more accurate conversion is necessary to produce a balanced recipe.*

Liquid measures *The millilitre has been used in this book and the following table gives a few examples.*

Imperial	Approx ml to nearest whole figure	Recommended ml
¼ pint	142	150 ml
½ pint	283	300 ml
¾ pint	425	450 ml
1 pint	567	600 ml
1½ pints	851	900 ml
1¾ pints	992	1000 ml (1 litre)

Spoon measures *All spoon measures given in this book are level unless otherwise stated.*

Can sizes *At present, cans are marked with the exact (usually to the nearest whole number) metric equivalent of the Imperial weight of the contents, so we have followed this practice when giving can sizes.*

Oven temperatures

The table below gives recommended equivalents.

	°C	°F	Gas Mark
Very cool	110	225	¼
	120	250	½
Cool	140	275	1
	150	300	2
Moderate	160	325	3
	180	350	4
Moderately hot	190	375	5
	200	400	6
Hot	220	425	7
	230	450	8
Very hot	240	475	9

Notes for American and Australian users

In America the 8-oz measuring cup is used. In Australia metric measures are now used in conjunction with the standard 250-ml measuring cup. The Imperial pint, used in Britain and Australia, is 20 fl oz, while the American pint is 16 fl oz. It is important to remember that the Australian tablespoon differs from both the British and American tablespoons; the table below gives a comparison. The British standard tablespoon, which has been used throughout this book, holds 17·7 ml, the American 14·2 ml, and the Australian 20 ml. A teaspoon holds approximately 5 ml in all three countries.

British	American	Australian
1 teaspoon	1 teaspoon	1 teaspoon
1 tablespoon	1 tablespoon	1 tablespoon
2 tablespoons	3 tablespoons	2 tablespoons
3½ tablespoons	4 tablespoons	3 tablespoons
4 tablespoons	5 tablespoons	3½ tablespoons

An Imperial/American guide to solid and liquid measures

Solid measures

IMPERIAL	AMERICAN
1 lb butter or margarine	2 cups
1 lb flour	4 cups
1 lb granulated or castor sugar	2 cups
1 lb icing sugar	3 cups
8 oz rice	1 cup

Liquid measures

IMPERIAL	AMERICAN
¼ pint liquid	⅔ cup liquid
½ pint	1¼ cups
¾ pint	2 cups
1 pint	2½ cups
1½ pints	3¾ cups
2 pints	5 cups (2½ pints)

NOTE: WHEN MAKING ANY OF THE RECIPES IN THIS BOOK, ONLY FOLLOW ONE SET OF MEASURES AS THEY ARE NOT INTERCHANGEABLE.

Introduction

For hundreds of years, people have looked forward to fresh food as it came into season. In the days when salted meat and fish and dried vegetables were the main winter diet, there was a particular welcome for the first spring vegetables, early lamb and duckling. Later there were the bountiful summer fruits and vegetables, and the rich autumn harvest.

Today, thanks to refrigeration and modern methods of food preservation, we can enjoy almost every kind of food on every day of the year, and yet fresh food in its due season still exerts powerful charm. We can mark the passage of the seasons by the appearance of the first green peas to go with the Whitsun duck, to be followed by gooseberry fool. Wimbledon is remembered as much for the strawberries served there as for the tennis which is played. In the summer holidays, we can enjoy shellfish fresh from the sea, and in the autumn the children benefit from expeditions to pick blackberries and mushrooms.

Not only are these foods delicious, but they are economical to use in their due season, when they are in plentiful supply. Not only will a seasonal menu be more appetising for family and guests, but it will also represent sound kitchen practice, making the most of 'glut' produce and of foods which seem to go together naturally.

Before each month's recipes, I have suggested the foods which will be in maximum supply during that time. This means that they should not only be of high quality, but also relatively inexpensive, which makes them suitable for freezing, or making into pickles or jams. Of course, many fresh foods are in season for two or three months, so you will be able to interchange some of the recipes when making up meal plans.

Today, many of us have freezers, so there will always be 'out-of-season' foods available, and we can make up raspberry dishes just as well in December as in July, and seafood is not just confined to the summer months, if you find that some recipes become family favourites and they want to eat them all the year round. In the same way, modern growing methods and improved transport guarantee us such 'out-of-season' vegetables as cucumbers or pineapples whenever we want them, so these have not been included in our monthly selection except in periods when they are likely to be very cheap.

All the recipes in this book are very easy to prepare and have been double-tested by me, and by Carol Bowen who prepared all the dishes for the photographs. We hope you enjoy them and find them an inspiration when faced with quantities of home produce or a glut of seasonal foods in the shops or on market stalls.

Mary Norwak

January

*This cold
month demands
warm nourishing food.
Root vegetables are at their best,
so this is a good time to make soups and
stews. There are plenty of apples and oranges
too for savoury dishes, puddings and cakes.
These winter dishes can be baked
together in the oven
to save fuel.*

Foods in Season

FISH

Carp · Cod · Haddock · Halibut · Herring · Mackerel · Mussels · Oysters · Pike · Plaice Scallops · Skate · Sole · Sprats · Whiting

POULTRY AND GAME

Chicken · Duck · Goose · Turkey · Hare · Partridge · Pheasant · Pigeon · Plover · Rabbit Snipe · Wild duck · Woodcock

VEGETABLES
(home produced and imported)

Broccoli · Brussels sprouts · Cabbage · Carrots · Cauliflower · Celery · Chicory · Jerusalem artichokes · Leeks · Parsnips · Red cabbage · Turnips · Watercress

FRUIT
(home produced and imported)

Cranberries · Grapefruit · Lemons · Oranges · Rhubarb · Seville oranges

Freezer Notes

There is little fresh food to freeze at the beginning of the year, so it is worth filling freezer space with casseroles and puddings for the remaining winter months. Citrus fruit is worth packing in dry sugar to freeze for breakfast or a refreshing sweet course. Seville oranges can be frozen whole without preparation for future marmalade-making. This is the last chance to buy game for the freezer.

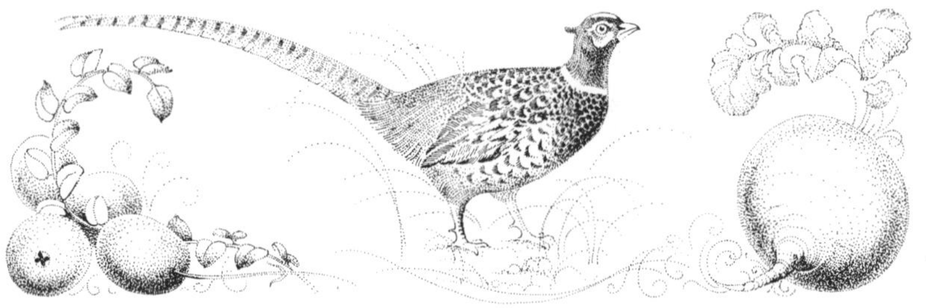

Soups and Starters

Cheese and Onion Soup

METRIC	IMPERIAL
2 rashers streaky bacon	2 rashers streaky bacon
225 g onion, sliced	8 oz onion, sliced
25 g butter	1 oz butter
15 g plain flour	½ oz plain flour
900 ml milk	1½ pints milk
salt and pepper	salt and pepper
50 g blue cheese	2 oz blue cheese
pinch of paprika	pinch of paprika

Remove the bacon rinds and chop the bacon finely. Put in a pan and heat gently to extract the fat. Stir in the onions and butter and cook slowly, stirring well until the onions are soft but not coloured. Sprinkle in the flour and cook for 1 minute. Gradually add the milk, salt and pepper. Bring to the boil, then reduce the heat and simmer for 10 minutes. Put through a sieve or purée in a liquidiser. Reheat to boiling point. Crumble the cheese finely into a tureen. Pour on the soup and sprinkle with paprika if liked. Serves 4

Cheese and Onion Soup *Artichoke and Shrimp Soup* *Minestrone*

Artichoke and Shrimp Soup

METRIC	IMPERIAL
675 g Jerusalem artichokes	1½ lb Jerusalem artichokes
50 g butter	2 oz butter
1 large onion, chopped	1 large onion, chopped
600 ml water	1 pint water
600 ml milk	1 pint milk
salt and pepper	salt and pepper
1 egg	1 egg
4 tablespoons double cream	4 tablespoons double cream
100 g peeled shrimps	4 oz peeled shrimps
1 tablespoon chopped parsley to garnish	1 tablespoon chopped parsley to garnish

Peel the artichokes thinly and slice them. Melt the butter and cook the onion until soft but not coloured. Add the artichokes and stir over gentle heat for 8 minutes. Add the water, bring to the boil and then simmer for 15 minutes. Put through a sieve or purée in a liquidiser. Return to the pan with the milk and seasoning, and simmer for 5 minutes.

Beat the egg and cream together and mix with a little of the hot liquid. Stir into the remaining soup. Stir in the shrimps and heat gently without boiling. Serve sprinkled with parsley. Serves 4

Minestrone

This soup makes a complete meal if served with some crusty or wholemeal bread. The vegetables may be a mixture of fresh, canned and frozen, according to availability.

METRIC	IMPERIAL
75 g dried haricot beans	3 oz dried haricot beans
1·75 litres beef or bacon stock	3 pints beef or bacon stock
100 g smoked bacon	4 oz smoked bacon
1 large carrot, sliced	1 large carrot, sliced
225 g potatoes, cubed	8 oz potatoes, cubed
1 medium onion, sliced	1 medium onion, sliced
¼ small cabbage, shredded	¼ small cabbage, shredded
1 clove garlic, crushed	1 clove garlic, crushed
1 (227-g) can tomatoes	1 (8-oz) can tomatoes
100 g frozen peas	4 oz frozen peas
pinch of dried rosemary	pinch of dried rosemary
salt and pepper	salt and pepper
75 g pasta	3 oz pasta
1 tablespoon chopped parsley	1 tablespoon chopped parsley
grated Parmesan cheese to sprinkle	grated Parmesan cheese to sprinkle

Cover the beans with water and leave to soak overnight. Drain the beans and put into a pan with the stock. Bring to the boil, then cover and simmer for 1½ hours. Chop the bacon into small pieces and heat in a small pan until the fat runs and the bacon is golden brown. Drain off the fat, and add the bacon to the stock. Add the prepared vegetables, garlic and tomatoes with their juice. Cover and simmer for 35 minutes.

Stir in the peas, rosemary, salt and pepper, and simmer for 5 minutes. Add the pasta shapes or small pieces of macaroni and cook for 12 minutes. Serve sprinkled with parsley and plenty of cheese. Serves 4–6

Top: Turkey Terrine served with Cranberry Sauce; bottom: Smoked Roe Mousse

Turkey Terrine

This is a good way of using the remains of the Christmas turkey and its trimmings. It may be eaten like a hot meat loaf with gravy, or served cold in slices like a pâté with salad.

METRIC	IMPERIAL
450 g cooked turkey	1 lb cooked turkey
450 g pork sausagemeat	1 lb pork sausagemeat
225 g poultry stuffing (see note)	8 oz poultry stuffing (see note)
150 ml thick gravy	¼ pint thick gravy

Cut the turkey in small thick slices, and mix the light and dark meat. Make up the poultry stuffing which should be well flavoured with herbs. Use a straight-sided ovenproof dish and grease it well. Put a layer of half the sausagemeat on the base. Top with half the turkey and half the stuffing, moistening the stuffing with a little gravy. Add another layer of sausagemeat and then turkey and stuffing and the remaining gravy. Cover with a piece of kitchen foil and bake in a moderate oven (180°C, 350°F, Gas Mark 4) for 1¼ hours. Remove the foil and continue cooking for 15 minutes. Serve hot in wedges with gravy and cranberry sauce. If preferred, cool under weights for 8 hours, then turn out and cut in slices or wedges. Serves 8

Note For this dish you can use the stuffing which has been cooked in the turkey, or, if there is not enough, use a packet of stuffing and make it up according to the manufacturer's instructions.

Smoked Roe Mousse

METRIC	IMPERIAL
350 g smoked cod's roe	12 oz smoked cod's roe
juice of ½ lemon	juice of ½ lemon
1 tablespoon olive oil	1 tablespoon olive oil
1 clove garlic, crushed	1 clove garlic, crushed
pepper	pepper
150 ml double cream	¼ pint double cream

Scrape the roe from its skin into a bowl (or use roe from a jar). Stir in the lemon juice, oil, garlic, pepper and cream. Put into a liquidiser and blend until light and fluffy. Spoon or pipe into individual serving dishes and chill. Sprinkle with finely chopped parsley if liked before serving with fingers of toast. Serves 4–6

Main Dishes

Kipper Cakes

METRIC	IMPERIAL
225 g cooked kippers	8 oz cooked kippers
225 g mashed potato	8 oz mashed potato
1 tablespoon chopped parsley	1 tablespoon chopped parsley
25 g butter, softened	1 oz butter, softened
salt and pepper	salt and pepper
2 eggs	2 eggs
50 g dry breadcrumbs	2 oz dry breadcrumbs

Remove skin and bones from the kippers and flake the flesh. Mix into the potato with the parsley, butter, salt and pepper. Beat the eggs lightly and use a little egg to bind the mixture so that it just holds together. Coat with the remaining egg and then with breadcrumbs. Fry in shallow fat or oil until crisp and golden. Serve hot with vegetables or with scrambled eggs. Serves 4

Steak, Kidney and Mushroom Pudding

METRIC	IMPERIAL
350 g self-raising flour	12 oz self-raising flour
pinch of salt	pinch of salt
175 g shredded suet	6 oz shredded suet
675 g chuck steak, cubed	$1\frac{1}{2}$ lb chuck steak, cubed
225 g ox kidney, chopped	8 oz ox kidney, chopped
100 g mushrooms, sliced	4 oz mushrooms, sliced
salt and pepper	salt and pepper

Mix the flour, salt and suet. Add just enough cold water to make a soft but not sticky dough. Mix the steak, kidney and mushrooms and sprinkle with a little salt, pepper and flour. Use two-thirds of the pastry to line a 1·5-litre/$2\frac{1}{2}$-pint pudding basin. Put in the meat and mushrooms and half-fill with cold water. Roll the remaining pastry to make a lid. Put on top of the meat and seal the edges carefully. Cover with a piece of greaseproof paper and then kitchen foil, and tie with string. Stand the basin in a saucepan and add boiling water to come halfway up the basin. Cover and boil for $4\frac{1}{2}$ hours, adding more boiling water to the pan to prevent drying out. Serves 6

Oven Beef with Carrots and Parsley Dumplings

This is a new version of that old favourite, boiled beef and carrots. It is full of flavour as little liquid is used, and it is much more convenient to leave a dish cooking for a long time in the oven rather than on top of the stove.

METRIC	IMPERIAL
1·5 kg salt beef brisket	3 lb salt beef brisket
225 g carrots	8 oz carrots
225 g onions	8 oz onions
4 sticks celery	4 sticks celery
2 bay leaves	2 bay leaves
6 black peppercorns	6 black peppercorns
Dumplings	*Dumplings*
175 g self-raising flour	6 oz self-raising flour
1 teaspoon salt	1 teaspoon salt
2 teaspoons chopped parsley	2 teaspoons chopped parsley
75 g shredded suet	3 oz shredded suet

Soak the meat in cold water overnight and then drain well. Line a roasting tin with kitchen foil and put the meat in the centre. Clean the vegetables and cut them into large pieces. Put them round the meat. Add the bay leaves and peppercorns, and pour on 300 ml/½ pint water. Cover the meat with a large piece of foil, tucking the edges well under the rim of the tin. Cook in the centre of a moderately hot oven (400°C, 200°F, Gas Mark 6) for 1 hour 50 minutes.

Sift the flour and salt into a bowl and stir in the parsley and suet. Mix to a stiff dough with a little cold water. Divide the mixture into eight pieces and form them into balls. Remove the foil from the meat and put the dumplings on top of the vegetables. Cover again with the foil, and continue cooking for 40 minutes until the dumplings are well risen and cooked.

Slice the beef and arrange on a warm serving dish. Surround with the vegetables and dumplings, and serve with the liquid from the roasting tin. Serves 6–8

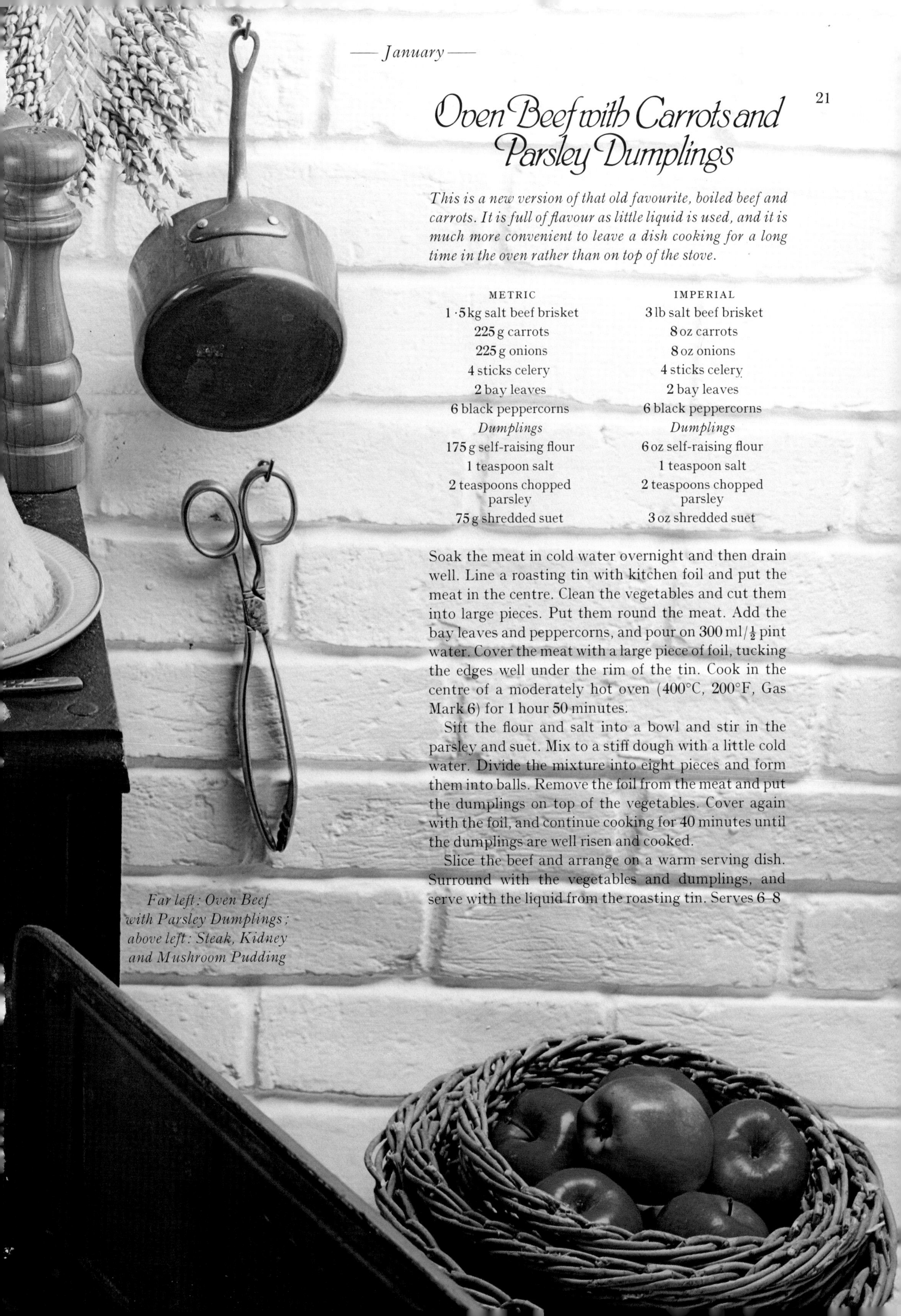

Far left: Oven Beef with Parsley Dumplings; above left: Steak, Kidney and Mushroom Pudding

Pot Roast Stuffed Lamb

METRIC	IMPERIAL
2 small onions, chopped	2 small onions, chopped
1 clove garlic, crushed	1 clove garlic, crushed
2 tablespoons chopped parsley	2 tablespoons chopped parsley
50 g fresh breadcrumbs	2 oz fresh breadcrumbs
1 tablespoon Worcestershire sauce	1 tablespoon Worcestershire sauce
salt and pepper	salt and pepper
150 ml stock	$\frac{1}{4}$ pint stock
1·5 kg shoulder of lamb, boned	3 lb shoulder of lamb, boned
1 tablespoon oil	1 tablespoon oil
150 ml dry cider	$\frac{1}{4}$ pint dry cider

Mix together the onions, garlic, parsley, breadcrumbs, sauce, salt and pepper and mix with a little stock to give a crumbly consistency. Stuff the lamb with this mixture and tie or skewer the meat to make a neat shape. Heat just enough oil or fat to grease the bottom of a pan, and brown the meat on all sides. Put into a casserole and add the remaining stock and cider. Season with salt and pepper. Cover and cook in a moderate oven (160°C, 325°F, Gas Mark 3) for $1\frac{3}{4}$ hours. The cooking liquid may be thickened with a little flour if liked, but it will reduce during cooking and taste delicious if just spooned over the joint. Serves 6–8

Baked Stuffed Liver

METRIC	IMPERIAL
675 g lamb's liver	$1\frac{1}{2}$ lb lamb's liver
25 g plain flour	1 oz plain flour
2 tablespoons fresh breadcrumbs	2 tablespoons fresh breadcrumbs
1 teaspoon chopped parsley	1 teaspoon chopped parsley
$\frac{1}{2}$ teaspoon salt	$\frac{1}{2}$ teaspoon salt
$\frac{1}{4}$ teaspoon pepper	$\frac{1}{4}$ teaspoon pepper
1 small onion, chopped	1 small onion, chopped
$\frac{1}{4}$ teaspoon grated lemon rind	$\frac{1}{4}$ teaspoon grated lemon rind
300 ml beef stock	$\frac{1}{2}$ pint beef stock
175 g bacon rashers	6 oz bacon rashers

Cut the liver in thin slices and toss in flour to coat them lightly. Arrange in a lightly greased shallow ovenproof dish. Mix together the breadcrumbs, parsley, salt, pepper, onion and lemon rind, and moisten with a little stock. Spread over the slices of liver and top with a layer of bacon rashers. Pour on the remaining stock, cover and bake in a moderately hot oven (190°C, 375°F, Gas Mark 5) for 40 minutes. Remove the lid and continue cooking for 10 minutes to make the bacon crisper. Serves 4–6

Pot Roast Stuffed Lamb *Baked Stuffed Liver*

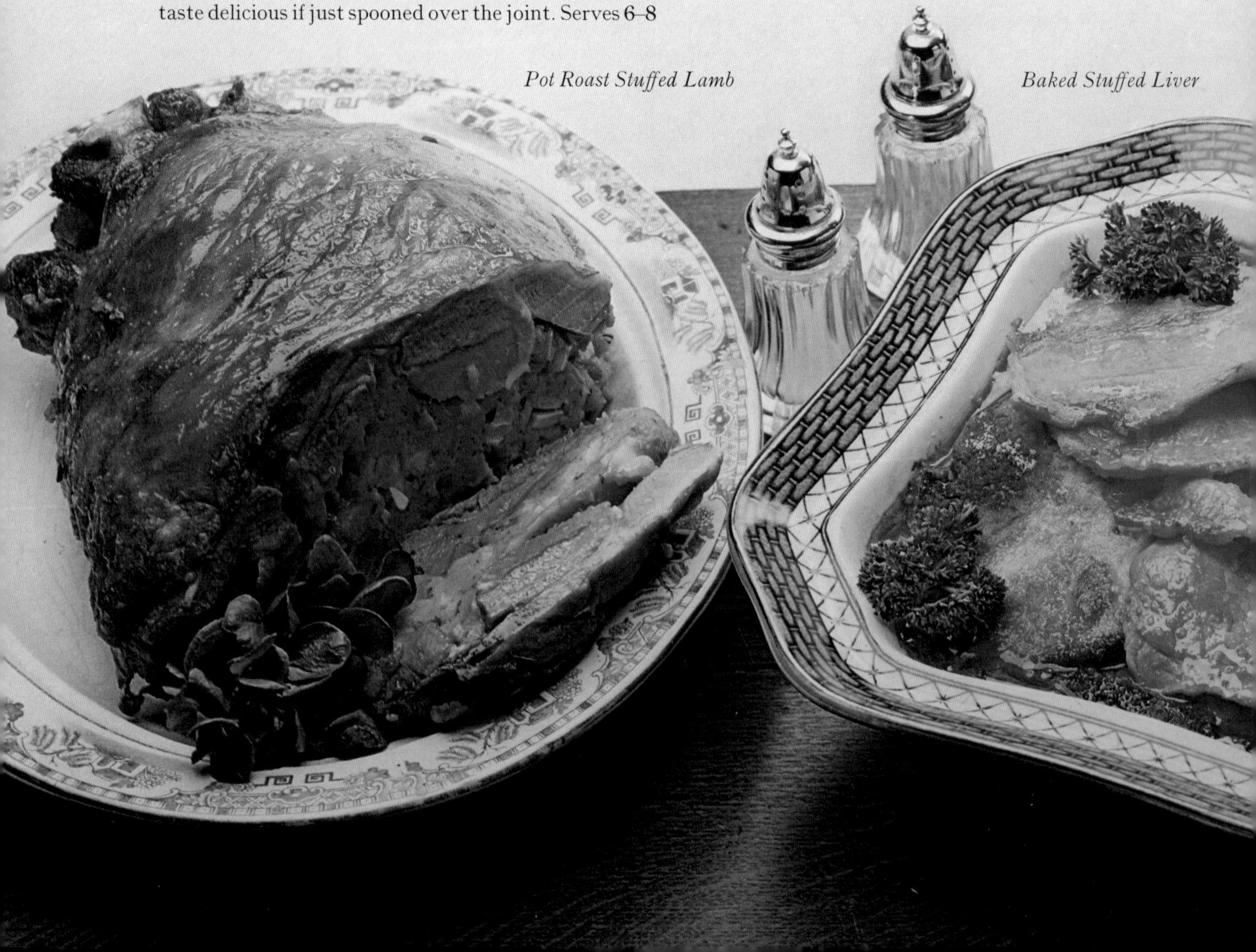

Pheasant and Apple Casserole

METRIC	IMPERIAL
1 pheasant	1 pheasant
450 g cooking apples	1 lb cooking apples
25 g butter	1 oz butter
225 g onions, sliced	8 oz onions, sliced
300 ml dry cider	½ pint dry cider
1 clove garlic, crushed	1 clove garlic, crushed
bunch of fresh mixed herbs	bunch of fresh mixed herbs
salt and pepper	salt and pepper

Clean and wipe the pheasant. Peel and core the apples and cut into quarters. Arrange the apples in the base of a casserole and put the pheasant on top of them. Melt the butter in a frying pan and cook the onions for 5 minutes until soft and golden. Put the onions on top of the pheasant, with the juices from the frying pan. Add the cider, garlic and herbs, and season well with salt and pepper. Cover and cook in a moderate oven (180°C, 350°F, Gas Mark 4) for 2 hours.

Remove the pheasant from the casserole and put it on a serving dish to keep warm. Remove the herbs from the casserole. Put the remaining contents through a sieve, or liquidise until smooth. Reheat and pour some of this sauce over the pheasant. Serve the remaining sauce in a sauceboat. Serves 4–6

Pheasant and Apple Casserole

Sweet Things

Ginger Marmalade Cake

METRIC	IMPERIAL
100 g butter	4 oz butter
50 g light soft brown sugar	2 oz light soft brown sugar
2 tablespoons golden syrup	2 tablespoons golden syrup
2 eggs	2 eggs
100 g self-raising flour	4 oz self-raising flour
¼ teaspoon baking powder	¼ teaspoon baking powder
½ teaspoon ground ginger	½ teaspoon ground ginger
6 tablespoons marmalade	6 tablespoons marmalade
icing sugar to dust	icing sugar to dust

Cream the butter, sugar and syrup until light and fluffy. Beat the eggs together and work into the creamed mixture. Sift the flour with the baking powder and ginger and fold into the creamed mixture. Put into two greased 18-cm/7-inch sandwich tins. Bake in a moderately hot oven (200°C, 400°F, Gas Mark 6) for 25 minutes. Turn out on to a wire rack to cool. Sandwich the cakes together with the marmalade and sift icing sugar over the top. Use orange, ginger or lemon marmalade, according to taste.

Ginger Marmalade Cake

Hazelnut Meringue Cake

METRIC	IMPERIAL
6 egg whites	6 egg whites
350 g castor sugar	12 oz castor sugar
75 g hazelnuts, chopped	3 oz hazelnuts, chopped
75 g ground almonds	3 oz ground almonds
Filling	*Filling*
175 g butter, softened	6 oz butter, softened
275 g icing sugar, sifted	10 oz icing sugar, sifted
75 g plain chocolate, melted	3 oz plain chocolate, melted
300 ml double cream	½ pint double cream

Whisk the egg whites to stiff peaks. Add half the sugar and continue beating until the mixture is stiff and glossy. Fold in the remaining sugar, hazelnuts and almonds.

Hazelnut Meringue Cake

1 · Base-line three 23-cm/9-inch sandwich tins with circles of parchment paper, and brush well with oil or melted fat.

2 · Spoon in the meringue mixture.

Bake in a moderate oven (160°C, 325°F, Gas Mark 3) for 40 minutes. Turn out on a wire rack and peel off the parchment paper. Leave until cold.

Beat the butter with the icing sugar and melted chocolate until light and creamy. Whip the cream to soft peaks.

3 · Put one meringue circle on a serving plate. Spread with half the chocolate mixture and top with half the cream. Put on the second meringue circle and spread with the remaining chocolate and cream. Top with the third meringue circle. Chill before serving. Serves 8

Orange Yogurt Cake

METRIC	IMPERIAL
175 g plain flour	6 oz plain flour
1½ teaspoons bicarbonate of soda	1½ teaspoons bicarbonate of soda
pinch of salt	pinch of salt
50 g butter	2 oz butter
300 g castor sugar	11 oz castor sugar
3 eggs	3 eggs
1 (142-ml) carton natural yogurt	1 (5-fl oz) carton natural yogurt
grated rind of 1 large orange	grated rind of 1 large orange
1 teaspoon lemon juice	1 teaspoon lemon juice
Icing	*Icing*
100 g icing sugar, sifted	4 oz icing sugar, sifted
1½ tablespoons orange juice	1½ tablespoons orange juice
slices of crystallised orange	slices of crystallised orange

Sift the flour, bicarbonate of soda and salt together. Cream the butter and work in the sugar. Separate the eggs and beat the yolks into the butter mixture. Add the yogurt, orange rind and lemon juice and gradually beat in the flour until thoroughly mixed. Whisk the egg whites to stiff peaks and fold into the mixture. Grease and base-line a 20-cm/8-inch round cake tin and put in the mixture.

Bake in a moderate oven (180°C, 350°F, Gas Mark 4) for 1¼ hours. Cool in the tin for 5 minutes, and turn out on a wire rack to cool. Mix the icing sugar and orange juice to give a smooth creamy icing. Spread the icing on top of the cake and decorate with crystallised orange slices.

Wholemeal Fruit Scones

METRIC	IMPERIAL
100 g wholemeal flour	4 oz wholemeal flour
100 g plain white flour	4 oz plain white flour
2 teaspoons baking powder	2 teaspoons baking powder
½ teaspoon salt	½ teaspoon salt
40 g butter	1½ oz butter
15 g castor sugar	½ oz castor sugar
25 g mixed dried fruit	1 oz mixed dried fruit
150 ml milk	¼ pint milk

Stir together the wholemeal and white flours, baking powder and salt. Rub in the butter and stir in the sugar and fruit. Mix to a soft dough with the milk. Roll out on a floured board to 1 cm/½ inch thick, and cut into 5-cm/2-inch rounds. Place on a baking tray close together. Brush the tops with a little milk. Bake in a hot oven (230°C, 450°F, Gas Mark 8) for 10 minutes. Cool on a wire rack.

Orange Yogurt Cake

Cranberry and Orange Plate Pie;
above: Wholemeal Fruit Scones

Cranberry and Orange Plate Pie

METRIC	IMPERIAL
350 g shortcrust pastry	12 oz shortcrust pastry
6 tablespoons water	6 tablespoons water
grated rind and juice of 1 large orange	grated rind and juice of 1 large orange
175 g light soft brown sugar	6 oz light soft brown sugar
225 g cranberries	8 oz cranberries
1 teaspoon cornflour	1 teaspoon cornflour
25 g butter	1 oz butter
castor sugar to sprinkle	castor sugar to sprinkle

Line an 18-cm/7-inch pie plate with half the pastry. Put the water, orange juice, orange rind and sugar into a pan and stir over low heat until the sugar has dissolved. Add the cranberries and simmer for 10 minutes until the skins pop and the fruit is soft. Mix the cornflour with a little water and stir into the fruit. Bring to the boil and stir until thick. Remove from the heat and stir in the butter. Cool and put into the pastry case.

Cover with the remaining pastry, sealing the edges firmly. Decorate with pastry leaves cut from the trimmings. Brush with a little milk and bake in a moderately hot oven (200°C, 400°F, Gas Mark 6) for 35 minutes. Sprinkle thickly with castor sugar before serving hot or cold.

February

Citrus fruit is very good now, so it is worth making marmalade to last for the year. The weather is so depressing that it is fun to make a special break to celebrate St. Valentine's Day, the feast of lovers, and Shrove Tuesday at the beginning of Lent, with traditional dishes.

Foods in Season

FISH

Carp · Cod · Haddock · Hake · Halibut · Herring · Mussels · Oysters · Pike · Plaice · Salmon
Scallops · Skate · Sole · Sprats · Whitebait

POULTRY AND GAME

Chicken · Duck · Goose · Turkey · Hare · Rabbit · Wild duck

VEGETABLES
(home produced and imported)

Broccoli · Brussels sprouts · Cabbage · Cauliflower · Celery · Chicory · Jerusalem artichokes
Leeks · Parsnips · Red cabbage · Turnips · Watercress

FRUIT
(home produced and imported)

Grapefruit · Lemons · Oranges · Rhubarb · Seville oranges

Freezer Notes

There is still time to freeze citrus fruit, and the last of the winter vegetables such as sprouts and celery. Early rhubarb is appearing in the shops and it is very delicate in flavour and worth preserving. The first imported lamb may be available for bulk buying. This is the end of the leek season, and they should be frozen for use in spring and summer soups.

Soups and Starters

Mussel Soup

METRIC	IMPERIAL
36 mussels in shells	36 mussels in shells
150 ml water	¼ pint water
50 g butter	2 oz butter
1 medium onion, chopped	1 medium onion, chopped
15 g plain flour	½ oz plain flour
1·15 litres milk	2 pints milk
salt and pepper	salt and pepper
1 (425-g) can tomatoes	1 (15-oz) can tomatoes

Scrub the mussels very thoroughly and remove any fibrous matter. Discard any which will not shut when tapped. Put into a large wide-bottomed pan and pour in the water. Cover and heat gently for 10 minutes, until the shells open. Discard any which do not open. Remove the mussels from their shells and chop each one in four pieces.

Melt the butter and cook the onion until soft but not browned. Stir in the flour and cook for 1 minute. Gradually stir in the milk and stir over a low heat for 10 minutes. Season well. Sieve the tomatoes and their liquid and add the purée to the milk. Stir in the mussels and simmer for 5 minutes. Serve very hot. Serves 6

Scallops Mornay

METRIC	IMPERIAL
8 scallops in shells	8 scallops in shells
1 teaspoon lemon juice	1 teaspoon lemon juice
300 ml cheese sauce	½ pint cheese sauce
50 g fresh breadcrumbs	2 oz fresh breadcrumbs
50 g Cheddar cheese, grated	2 oz Cheddar cheese, grated
25 g butter	1 oz butter

Remove the scallops from the shells and put them into a saucepan with the lemon juice and just enough water to cover. Poach for 10 minutes and then drain thoroughly. Wash and dry four of the deep scallop shells and arrange them on a baking tray. Spoon half of the cheese sauce into the shells. Sprinkle with half the breadcrumbs and arrange two scallops in each shell. Cover with the remaining sauce. Mix the remaining breadcrumbs with the cheese and sprinkle on top. Cut the butter into thin flakes and arrange on top of the breadcrumbs. Bake in a moderate oven (180°C, 350°F, Gas Mark 4) for 20 minutes. Serve very hot. Serves 4

Mussel Soup

Main Dishes

Mince and Vegetable Farmhouse Bake

METRIC	IMPERIAL
450 g fresh minced beef	1 lb fresh minced beef
225 g mixed vegetables, cooked	8 oz mixed vegetables, cooked
450 ml gravy	$\frac{3}{4}$ pint gravy
1 tablespoon tomato ketchup	1 tablespoon tomato ketchup
salt and pepper	salt and pepper
450 g potatoes	1 lb potatoes
25 g butter	1 oz butter
150 ml milk	$\frac{1}{4}$ pint milk
25 g Cheddar cheese, grated	1 oz Cheddar cheese, grated

Put the minced beef into a thick pan and heat gently until the fat runs and the meat is lightly coloured. Drain off any surplus fat. Stir the vegetables into the meat with the gravy, tomato ketchup, salt and pepper. The vegetables can be whatever is available, and they are best cut into small cubes before mixing with the meat. Simmer, stirring for 10 minutes, and then put into an ovenproof dish.

Peel the potatoes and cook them until just tender. Heat the butter and milk to boiling point. Drain the potatoes and pour in the butter and milk. Beat well until the potatoes are light and creamy. Season to taste. Spread the potatoes on the meat mixture and sprinkle with cheese. Bake in a moderate oven (180°C, 350°F, Gas Mark 4) for 40 minutes. Serve hot with some extra gravy. Serves 4

Scallops Mornay

Pork and Red Cabbage Casserole

Red cabbage is often eaten pickled in vinegar, but it makes a superb hot vegetable which is particularly good with rich meats such as pork, goose, ham or sausages.

METRIC	IMPERIAL
1 medium red cabbage	1 medium red cabbage
100 g butter	4 oz butter
4 large cooking apples	4 large cooking apples
1 large onion, sliced	1 large onion, sliced
2 cloves garlic, crushed	2 cloves garlic, crushed
$\frac{1}{4}$ teaspoon grated nutmeg	$\frac{1}{4}$ teaspoon grated nutmeg
$\frac{1}{4}$ teaspoon ground allspice	$\frac{1}{4}$ teaspoon ground allspice
$\frac{1}{4}$ teaspoon caraway seed	$\frac{1}{4}$ teaspoon caraway seed
salt and pepper	salt and pepper
grated rind of 1 orange	grated rind of 1 orange
25 g light soft brown sugar	1 oz light soft brown sugar
450 ml red wine	$\frac{3}{4}$ pint red wine
2 tablespoons wine vinegar	2 tablespoons wine vinegar
4 tablespoons water	4 tablespoons water
4 pork chops	4 pork chops

Cut the cabbage into quarters. Cut out the heavy ribs and stalk, and discard. Shred the cabbage coarsely. Melt the butter in a heavy pan. Put in the cabbage and cover with a lid. Cook for 10 minutes, stirring once. Peel the apples, remove the cores, and cut the apples into quarters.

Put half the cabbage and its juices into a casserole. Top with half the onions and apples. Add half the garlic, and sprinkle on half the nutmeg, allspice, caraway seed, salt, pepper and orange rind. Put in the remaining cabbage, onion, apple, spices and orange rind. Sprinkle on the brown sugar and then add the wine, vinegar and water.

Cover and cook in a moderately hot oven (190°C, 375°F, Gas Mark 5) for 45 minutes. Grill the pork chops for 5 minutes on each side under a hot grill. Arrange on top of the casseroled cabbage. Cover and continue cooking in the oven for 15 minutes. Serve very hot. Serves 4

Chicken Pudding

METRIC	IMPERIAL
350 g self-raising flour	12 oz self-raising flour
175 g shredded suet	6 oz shredded suet
pinch of salt	pinch of salt
1 boiling chicken	1 boiling chicken
1 medium onion, chopped	1 medium onion, chopped
1 clove garlic, crushed	1 clove garlic, crushed
salt and pepper	salt and pepper
1 tablespoon chopped parsley	1 tablespoon chopped parsley
1 bay leaf	1 bay leaf

Stir the flour and suet together with a pinch of salt. Add just enough cold water to make a firm dough. Roll out the dough on a floured board and use two-thirds of it to line a 1-litre/2-pint pudding basin. Remove the skin from the bird, and cut off the flesh in neat pieces. Put the skin and bones into 1·75 litres/3 pints water and simmer to make stock.

Put a layer of chicken into the basin. Top with a little onion, garlic, salt, pepper and parsley. Put on another layer of chicken and add the bay leaf. Top with onion, garlic, salt, pepper and parsley and finish with a layer of chicken. Add enough of the chicken stock or water to cover the meat. Put on a lid of the remaining suet dough and seal the edges well. Cover with a piece of greaseproof paper and then kitchen foil. Tie firmly and put the basin into a large pan with water to come half-way up the sides. Cover and boil for 4 hours, adding boiling water so that the pan does not dry out. Turn out and serve with gravy made from the chicken stock, or parsley sauce. Serves 6

Note: This dish can be made using cooked chicken. In this case, reduce the steaming time to 2 hours.

Pork and Red Cabbage Casserole

Chicken Pudding

Surprise Cheese Soufflé

Surprise Cheese Soufflé

There really is a surprise in this soufflé, as it has lightly cooked eggs in the centre. Is is very rich and delicious, but easy to make. All soufflés must be taken straight to the table to eat while very hot and puffy.

METRIC	IMPERIAL
75 g butter	3 oz butter
50 g plain flour	2 oz plain flour
300 ml milk	½ pint milk
salt and pepper	salt and pepper
½ teaspoon dry mustard	½ teaspoon dry mustard
100 g Cheddar cheese, grated	4 oz Cheddar cheese, grated
7 eggs	7 eggs

Prepare a soufflé dish before starting the recipe. Use a 1-litre/2-pint dish and grease it with a little olive oil.

Melt the butter and sift in the flour, stirring well. Gradually add the milk and stir over a low heat until smooth and creamy. Season well. Remove from the heat and stir in the mustard and cheese. Separate 3 of the eggs. Beat the yolks thoroughly and work into the cheese mixture. Whisk the whites to stiff peaks.

Fold the egg whites into the cheese mixture. Put half the mixture into the prepared dish. Break the remaining eggs on top so that they are evenly spaced. Very carefully, spoon the remaining cheese mixture on top. Bake in a moderately hot oven (190°C, 375°F, Gas Mark 5) for 45 minutes. Serve at once. Serves 4

Winter Crunchy Salad

Winter Crunchy Salad

A colourful and crisp winter salad makes a perfect accompaniment to hot or cold meals, and can be made with a small assortment of vegetables.

METRIC	IMPERIAL
225 g white cabbage	8 oz white cabbage
100 g red cabbage	4 oz red cabbage
100 g Brussels sprouts	4 oz Brussels sprouts
1 medium leek	1 medium leek
1 large carrot	1 large carrot
300 ml mayonnaise	½ pint mayonnaise
1 tablespoon wine vinegar	1 tablespoon wine vinegar
½ teaspoon dry mustard	½ teaspoon dry mustard
pinch of sugar	pinch of sugar
50 g walnuts, chopped	2 oz walnuts, chopped

Shred the white and red cabbage finely and put into a salad bowl. Trim off the stems and outer leaves from the sprouts, and cut the sprouts across in very thin slices. Trim the root and dark green top from the leek. Wash it very thoroughly, and then cut across in very thin slices. Grate the carrot coarsely. Put the sprouts, leek and carrot into the bowl.

Mix the mayonnaise with the vinegar, mustard and sugar. Stir into the bowl and mix the vegetables thoroughly. Sprinkle the walnuts on top. If liked, add a few pieces of celery or apple, or some watercress leaves. Serves 4–6

Sweet Things

Pancakes

Pancakes are traditionally eaten on Shrove Tuesday, the day before the beginning of Lent. They were made to use up the ingredients in the house before the days of fasting.

METRIC	IMPERIAL
100 g plain flour	4 oz plain flour
$\frac{1}{4}$ teaspoon salt	$\frac{1}{4}$ teaspoon salt
1 egg and 1 egg yolk	1 egg and 1 egg yolk
300 ml milk	$\frac{1}{2}$ pint milk
1 tablespoon oil or melted butter	1 tablespoon oil or melted butter
wedges of lemon	wedges of lemon
castor sugar to sprinkle	castor sugar to sprinkle

Sift the flour and salt together and mix in the egg and egg yolk and a little of the milk. Beat together and gradually beat in the remaining milk to make a smooth batter. Fold in the oil or melted butter.

Use an 18-cm/7-inch frying pan with a rounded base to fry the pancakes. Heat the pan and wipe it over with a piece of greased paper, just enough to make the base of the pan shine. Pour in a little batter and quickly tilt the pan so that the batter spreads over the surface. Cook until the top of the batter has just set, and turn the pancake with a palette knife. Cook until just golden. Lift on to a hot serving dish and fold in three. Repeat the greasing and cooking process, keeping the cooked pancakes warm. Serve at once with lemon and sugar.

Various other fillings can be added to the cooked pancakes. Keep them warm unfolded and roll them up around a hot filling of jam, stewed fruit or chopped nuts mixed with honey or maple syrup. (If liked, pancakes can be cooked in advance and can be frozen, layered with greaseproof paper, for later use.) Serves 4

Orange Fruit Pudding with Orange Sauce

METRIC	IMPERIAL
100 g white bread	4 oz white bread
4 tablespoons orange marmalade	4 tablespoons orange marmalade
4 tablespoons orange juice	4 tablespoons orange juice
50 g butter	2 oz butter
50 g sugar	2 oz sugar
1 egg	1 egg
75 g self-raising flour	3 oz self-raising flour
100 g sultanas	4 oz sultanas
Sauce	*Sauce*
juice of 2 oranges	juice of 2 oranges
150 ml water	$\frac{1}{4}$ pint water
1 tablespoon cornflour	1 tablespoon cornflour
sugar to taste	sugar to taste

Break the bread into small pieces and put into a bowl. Heat the marmalade and orange juice until the marmalade has melted, and pour on to the bread. Leave for 30 minutes until the bread is very soft. Cream the butter and sugar until light and fluffy. Work in the egg and flour until well mixed, and then stir in the sultanas. Add the bread mixture and beat well. Put into a greased 1-litre/$1\frac{1}{2}$-pint pudding basin and cover with greaseproof paper and kitchen foil. Put into a pan with boiling water to halfway up the basin. Cover and boil for 2 hours, adding more boiling water so that the pan does not dry out. Turn out and serve with orange sauce. To make the sauce, heat the orange juice and water. Mix the cornflour with a little water and stir into the orange juice and water. Reheat and stir until creamy, adding a little sugar if liked. Serves 4

Winter Dried Fruit Salad

METRIC	IMPERIAL
225 g prunes	8 oz prunes
225 g dried apricots	8 oz dried apricots
100 g dried apples and pears	4 oz dried apples and pears
slice of lemon	slice of lemon
450 ml sweet cider	$\frac{3}{4}$ pint sweet cider
50 g mixed nuts, chopped	2 oz mixed nuts, chopped

Put the prunes, apricots, apples and pears into a bowl. Cover with cold water and leave to soak for 8 hours. Drain very thoroughly. Put the fruit into a pan with the lemon and cider. Bring to the boil and then simmer for 45 minutes. Stir in the nuts. Serve hot or cold with cream. Serves 4–6

Orange Fruit Pudding with Orange Sauce; Winter Dried Fruit Salad

St. Valentine Cake

Valentine's Day is celebrated by lovers on February 14th, the day on which the birds begin to build their nests. This heart-shaped cake will appeal to any man.

METRIC	IMPERIAL
3 eggs	3 eggs
175 g castor sugar	6 oz castor sugar
2 tablespoons strong black coffee	2 tablespoons strong black coffee
175 g plain flour	6 oz plain flour
Icing	*Icing*
125 g butter	5 oz butter
225 g icing sugar	8 oz icing sugar
3 tablespoons strong black coffee	3 tablespoons strong black coffee
Caramel	*Caramel*
100 g cube sugar	4 oz cube sugar
150 ml water	$\frac{1}{4}$ pint water

Separate the eggs and put the yolks into a bowl with the sugar and coffee. Put the bowl over a pan of hot water and whisk until thick and fluffy. Remove the

St. Valentine Cake

bowl from the pan and whisk again for 1 minute. Sift the flour. Whisk the egg whites to stiff peaks. Fold the flour into the yolk mixture, then fold in the egg whites. Put into a greased 20-cm/8-inch heart-shaped tin. Bake in a moderate oven (180°C, 350°F, Gas Mark 4) for 45 minutes. Turn out and cool on a wire rack.

To make the icing, beat the butter until soft and fluffy. Sift the icing sugar and beat into the butter with the coffee. Cut the cake in half and sandwich together with some of the icing. Spread nearly all the remaining icing over the top and sides to cover the cake. Use the rest to pipe small stars round the top of the cake.

To make the caramel, dissolve the sugar in the water and then boil rapidly until dark golden brown. Pour out of the pan at once on to a sheet of greaseproof paper and leave to cool and harden. Crack into small pieces with a rolling pin and use to decorate the top of the cake.

Baking

Soda Bread

It is very quick to make this bread, and no yeast is needed. It is usually cooked on a hot griddle, but a thick frying pan may be used instead. Soda bread is very good with a salad meal, or may be eaten at breakfast with plenty of butter.

METRIC	IMPERIAL
225 g wholemeal flour	8 oz wholemeal flour
225 g plain white flour	8 oz plain white flour
2 teaspoons light soft brown sugar	2 teaspoons light soft brown sugar
1 teaspoon bicarbonate of soda	1 teaspoon bicarbonate of soda
1 teaspoon salt	1 teaspoon salt
1 tablespoon soft dripping	1 tablespoon soft dripping
milk to bind	milk to bind

Stir together the wholemeal and white flours and add the sugar, soda and salt. Rub in the dripping. Add just enough milk to make a stiff dough. Roll out on a lightly floured board to a 2·5-cm/1-inch thick round. Mark deeply with a knife to form a cross. Flour a griddle or thick frying pan very lightly and heat the griddle. Put on the bread and cook for 10 minutes each side. Put on a wire rack to cool slightly, but eat while freshly cooked.

Preserves

Old-Fashioned Marmalade

METRIC	IMPERIAL
1·4 kg Seville oranges	3 lb Seville oranges
1 lemon	1 lemon
3 litres water	5 pints water
2·75 kg sugar	6 lb sugar
1 tablespoon black treacle	1 tablespoon black treacle

Cut the oranges in half and squeeze the juice into a preserving pan. Squeeze the lemon juice into the pan. Put the pips from the fruit in a muslin bag. Cut the orange rind into thick shreds. Put into the pan with the bag of pips and the water. Simmer for 2 hours until the peel is tender. Remove the bag of pips and squeeze the liquid back into the pan.

Add the sugar with the black treacle over a low heat and stir until it has dissolved. Bring to the boil and boil rapidly until setting point is reached (a spoonful of the mixture put on a cold plate will set quickly and will wrinkle when pushed gently with a finger). Cool for 15 minutes and stir well to distribute the peel. Put into clean jars and cover with a waxed disc and top cover.

Three-Fruit Marmalade

This marmalade has a most unusual flavour, and it is a useful preserve to make all through the year when the traditional Seville oranges are not available.

METRIC	IMPERIAL
2 grapefruit	2 grapefruit
2 sweet oranges	2 sweet oranges
4 lemons	4 lemons
3·5 litres water	6 pints water
2·75 kg sugar	6 lb sugar

Cut all the fruit in half. Remove the pips and put them into a piece of muslin or clean cotton. Remove the flesh from the grapefruit and put into a preserving pan. Scrape out the grapefruit pith and membranes and put into the cloth with the pips. Tie the cloth into a bag and suspend it in the pan. Scoop out the flesh from the oranges and lemons and put into the pan. Shred all the peel finely.

Add the peel to the pan with the water and simmer for 1½ hours until the peel is tender. Take out the bag of pips and squeeze the liquid back into the pan. Stir in the sugar over a low heat until it has dissolved. Bring to the boil, and boil rapidly until setting point is reached (a spoonful of the mixture put on a cold plate will set quickly and will wrinkle when pushed gently with a finger). Cool for 15 minutes and stir well to distribute the peel. Put into clean jars and cover with a waxed disc and top cover.

Grapefruit Marmalade

METRIC	IMPERIAL
3 grapefruit	3 grapefruit
4 lemons	4 lemons
2·25 litres water	4 pints water
1·4 kg sugar	3 lb sugar

Cut the fruit in half and squeeze the juice into a preserving pan. Remove the pith and membranes from the grapefruit and put into a muslin bag with the pips from both fruit. Cut the grapefruit and lemon peel into medium thick shreds and put into the pan with the juice, water and bag of pips. Simmer for 1½ hours until the peel is tender. Remove the bag of pips and squeeze the liquid back into the pan.

Stir in the sugar over a low heat until it has dissolved. Bring to the boil and boil rapidly until setting point is reached (a spoonful of the mixture put on a cold plate will set quickly and will wrinkle when pushed gently with a finger). Cool for 15 minutes and stir well to distribute the peel. Put into clean jars and cover with a waxed disc and top cover.

Menu

FEBRUARY

Leeks Vinaigrette

Cheese Soufflé with Poached Eggs
Soda Bread
Winter Crunchy Salad

St. Valentine Cake

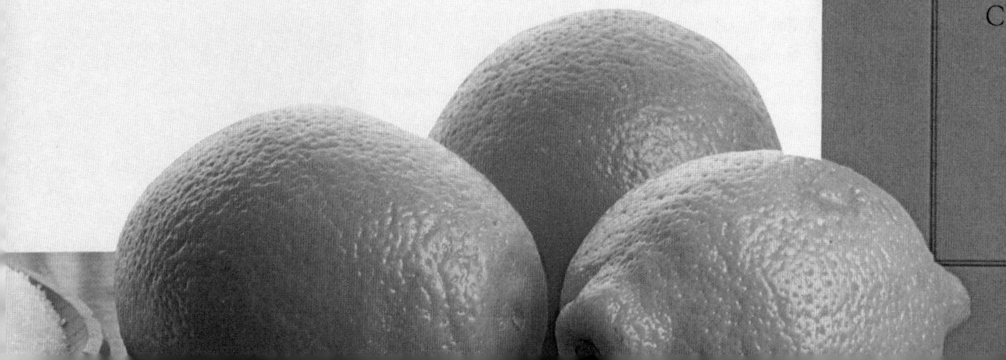

March

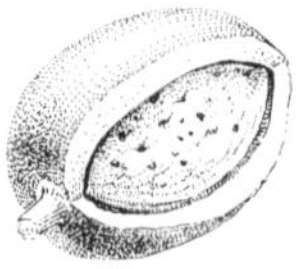

This is the beginning of Spring, so there are early vegetables to enjoy and the first lamb appears. Lemons are in good supply and it is fun to make refreshing curds and sorbets. The fourth Sunday in Lent is Mothering Sunday when a traditional almond-iced cake should be eaten.

Foods in Season

FISH

Carp · Hake · Halibut · Herring · Mackerel · Mussels · Oysters · Pike · Plaice · Salmon Salmon trout · Scallops · Skate · Sole · Sprats · Trout · Turbot · Whitebait

POULTRY AND GAME

Chicken · Duck · Goose · Turkey

VEGETABLES
(home produced and imported)

Broccoli · Brussels sprouts · Cabbage · Cauliflower · Celery · Chicory · Jerusalem artichokes Leeks · Parsnips

FRUIT
(home produced and imported)

Grapefruit · Lemons · Oranges · Rhubarb

Freezer Notes

This month is usually recognised as being the beginning of Spring when we can look forward to some delicious new food after the winter. The first salmon, English lamb and ducks are coming into season, and it may be worth keeping some in the freezer for a special treat. Early vegetables are appearing, such as broccoli and cauliflower, and rhubarb is growing in the garden. If there is time to spare, it is a good idea to freeze dishes for Easter and the first holiday period.

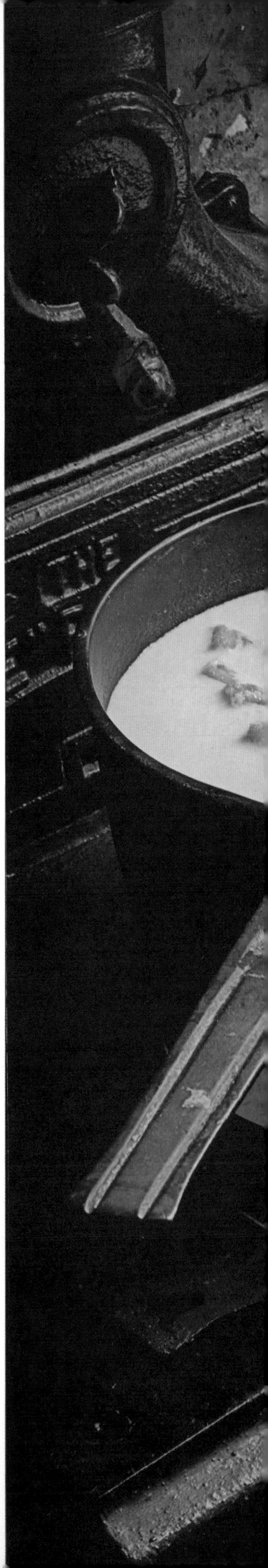

MINT
NUTMEG

Watercress Soup

Soups

Watercress Soup

METRIC	IMPERIAL
2 bunches watercress	2 bunches watercress
450 g potatoes	1 lb potatoes
50 g butter	2 oz butter
1 small onion, sliced	1 small onion, sliced
salt and pepper	salt and pepper
900 ml chicken stock	$1\frac{1}{2}$ pints chicken stock
300 ml single cream	$\frac{1}{2}$ pint single cream

Reserve a few watercress leaves for garnish. Chop the remaining leaves and stems. Peel and cube the potatoes. Melt the butter and add the onion and watercress. Season with salt and pepper and cover. Simmer over a low heat for 5 minutes. Add the potatoes, stir, cover and continue cooking over a low heat without browning for 15 minutes.

Boil the chicken stock and pour on to the vegetables. Stir well, bring to the boil and simmer for 20 minutes. Sieve or purée in a liquidiser. Return to a clean pan, check the seasoning and reheat. Stir in the cream and reheat very gently without boiling. Serve garnished with watercress leaves. Serves 4–6

Carrot Soup

METRIC	IMPERIAL
450 g carrots	1 lb carrots
600 ml water	1 pint water
3 large tomatoes	3 large tomatoes
25 g butter	1 oz butter
600 ml milk	1 pint milk
salt and pepper	salt and pepper
Garnish	*Garnish*
chopped parsley	chopped parsley
toast croûtons	toast croûtons

Scrape the carrots and cut them into small pieces. Put into a pan with the water, bring to the boil and simmer for 30 minutes with a lid on. Drain the carrots, reserving the liquid. Peel the tomatoes and remove the seeds. Melt the butter and simmer the tomatoes for 3 minutes. Add the carrot and cook for 3 minutes. Add the reserved carrot water and simmer for 10 minutes, stirring well.

Sieve or liquidise, and return to a clean pan with the milk. Simmer for 15 minutes and season to taste. Serve garnished with toast croûtons and parsley. Serves 4–6

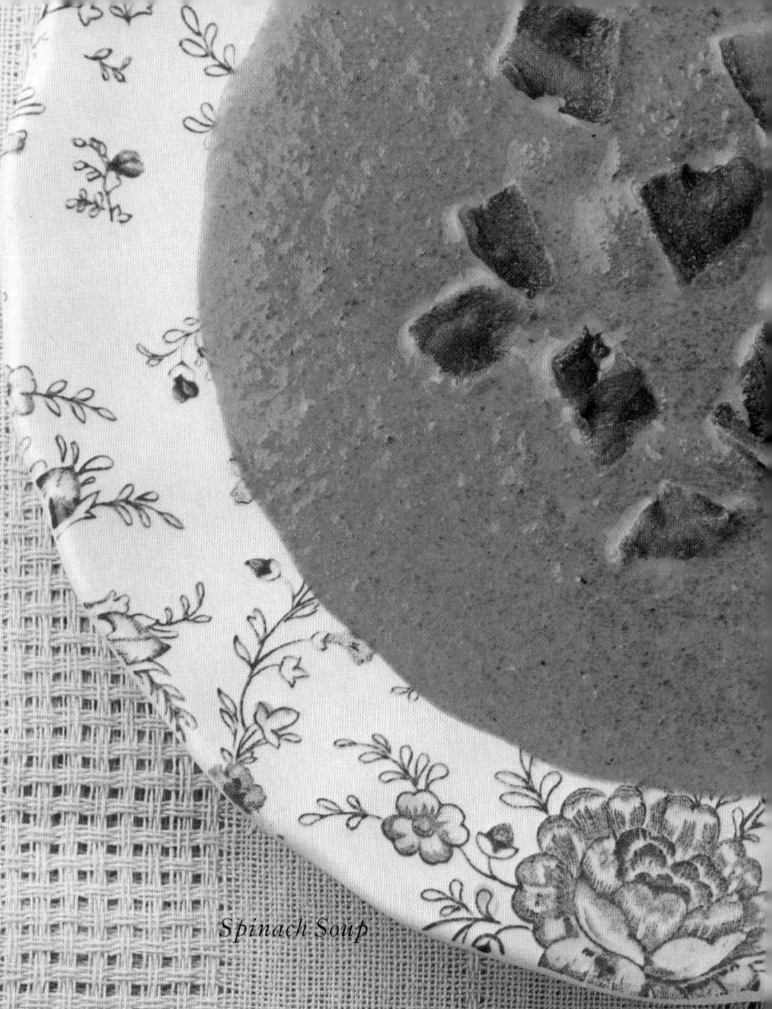

Spinach Soup

Carrot Soup

Spinach Soup

METRIC	IMPERIAL
1 kg fresh spinach	2 lb fresh spinach
1 medium onion, chopped	1 medium onion, chopped
1 small green pepper, chopped	1 small green pepper, chopped
50 g butter	2 oz butter
1 teaspoon sugar	1 teaspoon sugar
salt and pepper	salt and pepper
1 teaspoon dried tarragon	1 teaspoon dried tarragon
450 ml milk	¾ pint milk
150 ml single cream	¼ pint single cream

Strip the spinach leaves from the stems. Wash the leaves very well and drain. Put the onion and pepper into a pan with the butter and cook gently for 5 minutes. Stir in the spinach, sugar, salt, pepper and tarragon. Cover tightly and simmer for about 10 minutes until the spinach is tender.

Sieve or liquidise, and return to a clean pan. Stir in the milk and cream and reheat gently without boiling. If liked, serve garnished with small pieces of crisp bacon. Serves 4

Main Dishes

Smoked Haddock Kedgeree

This fish and rice dish was originally eaten for breakfast, but these days it is more appreciated as a light lunch or supper. Smoked haddock or smoked cod fillet are suitable, but left-over salmon is sometimes used.

METRIC	IMPERIAL
450 g smoked haddock, cooked and flaked	1 lb smoked haddock, cooked and flaked
225 g short-grain rice	8 oz short-grain rice
75 g butter	3 oz butter
salt and pepper	salt and pepper
1 tablespoon chopped parsley	1 tablespoon chopped parsley
2 eggs, hard-boiled and chopped	2 eggs, hard-boiled and chopped
pinch of curry powder	pinch of curry powder

Put the flaked fish into an ovenproof dish. Put the rice into a pan of fast-boiling salted water and boil for about 15 minutes until just tender. Drain very thoroughly. Stir the rice into the fish. Add the butter, cut into thin flakes. Add to the rice with the seasoning, parsley, eggs and curry powder. Mix well. Heat in a moderate oven (160°C, 325°F, Gas Mark 3) for 10 minutes. Stir well to distribute the butter and serve hot. Serves 4

Smoked Haddock Kedgeree

Lamb Cutlets in Pastry

These little parcels of lamb in pastry look very attractive for a dinner party, and they taste just as good when cold, so that they are suitable for a buffet, or even for a picnic.

METRIC	IMPERIAL
8 lamb cutlets	8 lamb cutlets
100 g mushrooms, chopped	4 oz mushrooms, chopped
1 small onion, chopped	1 small onion, chopped
25 g butter	1 oz butter
salt and pepper	salt and pepper
pinch of curry powder	pinch of curry powder
450 g frozen puff pastry	1 lb frozen puff pastry
beaten egg to glaze	beaten egg to glaze

Lamb Cutlets in Pastry

If lamb cutlets are not obtainable, use small loin chops, but be sure that a long piece of bone is left above the 'eye' of the meat. Scrape any fat and skin from the top 5 cm/2 inches of the bones. Wrap a piece of foil securely around the top of the bones to prevent colouring. Grill the chops on both sides until just cooked through but not browned. Leave until cold.

Cook the mushrooms and onion in the butter over a low heat until soft but not browned. Season well with salt, pepper and curry powder and leave until cold. Roll out the pastry thinly and cut into long 1-cm/½-inch strips. Put a little of the mushroom mixture on the centre of each cutlet. Starting at the bone tips, wind the pastry around each cutlet, overlapping slightly and sealing with beaten egg as you go. A quicker method is to wrap each cutlet in a square of pastry and decorate with pastry leaves.

Brush well with beaten egg to glaze the pastry. Bake in a hot oven (220°C, 425°F, Gas Mark 7) for 25 minutes until the pastry is crisp and golden. Serve hot with vegetables or cold with salad. Serves 4–6

Kidney and Sausage Surprise

METRIC	IMPERIAL
50 g butter	2 oz butter
6 lamb's kidneys	6 lamb's kidneys
1 large onion, chopped	1 large onion, chopped
100 g streaky bacon, chopped	4 oz streaky bacon, chopped
100 g button mushrooms	4 oz button mushrooms
15 g seasoned flour	½ oz seasoned flour
300 ml brown ale	½ pint brown ale
1 tablespoon tomato purée	1 tablespoon tomato purée
salt and pepper	salt and pepper
225 g chipolata sausages	8 oz chipolata sausages
300 ml soured cream	½ pint soured cream

Put half the butter into a pan. Skin the kidneys and remove the cores. Cut the kidneys in half. Heat the butter and cook the kidneys gently for 5 minutes, stirring often. Lift out the kidneys and keep them warm. Add the remaining butter to the pan and cook the onion, bacon and whole mushrooms over low heat for 5 minutes, stirring well. Stir in the flour, cook for 1 minute and then stir in the brown ale gradually. Bring to the boil, stirring well, and then stir in the tomato purée and seasoning. Simmer for 5 minutes, stirring well.

Meanwhile, grill the sausages until well browned and cooked through. Add the sausages and kidneys to the sauce. Remove from heat and stir in the soured cream. Reheat very gently, but do not boil. Serve with mashed potatoes. Serves 4

Kidney and Sausage Surprise

Vegetable Dishes

St. David's Leek Pie

The leek is a Welsh symbol, so March 1st (St. David's Day) can be celebrated with a simple leek pie which makes a good meal on its own, or which may be accompanied by hot or cold meat.

METRIC	IMPERIAL
225 g shortcrust pastry	8 oz shortcrust pastry
6 large leeks	6 large leeks
25 g butter	1 oz butter
300 ml creamy milk	½ pint creamy milk
2 eggs	2 eggs
salt and pepper	salt and pepper
25 g Cheddar cheese, grated	1 oz Cheddar cheese, grated

Line an 18-cm/7-inch sandwich tin with half the pastry. Trim the roots and green tops from the leeks. Wash the leeks thoroughly and cut them into thin slices. Melt the butter and cook the leeks gently until soft but not coloured. Cool to lukewarm and put into the pastry case. Beat the milk and eggs together until just blended and season well. Pour over the leeks and sprinkle with cheese. Cover with the remaining pastry and seal the edges firmly. Brush with a little extra milk. Bake in a moderately hot oven (200°C, 400°F, Gas Mark 6) for 40 minutes until golden. Serve hot. Serves 4–6

St. Patrick's Bacon

The patron saint of Ireland has his feast day on March 17th, and we can enjoy a dish made with bacon and potatoes, two favourite Irish products.

METRIC	IMPERIAL
675 g potatoes	1½ lb potatoes
2 large onions, sliced	2 large onions, sliced
salt and pepper	salt and pepper
1 egg	1 egg
300 ml milk	½ pint milk
25 g butter	1 oz butter
4 (100-g) rashers bacon	4 (4-oz) rashers bacon

Peel the potatoes and cut them into thin slices. Grease a casserole and put in alternate layers of potatoes and onions, seasoning well with salt and pepper. Finish with a layer of potatoes. Beat the egg and milk together until well mixed and pour over the potatoes and onions. Dot with flakes of butter.

The bacon rashers should be cut thickly so that each person has one. Trim off the rind and snip the fat so that the rashers will not curl. Put the bacon in a layer on top of the potatoes. Cover and cook in a moderate oven (180°C, 350°F, Gas Mark 4) for 1 hour. Remove the lid and continue cooking for 15 minutes. Serves 4

Broccoli and Ham in Cheese Sauce

METRIC	IMPERIAL
8 broccoli spears	8 broccoli spears
8 thin slices cooked ham	8 thin slices cooked ham
600 ml cheese sauce	1 pint cheese sauce
salt and pepper	salt and pepper
25 g fresh white breadcrumbs	1 oz fresh white breadcrumbs
25 g butter, softened	1 oz butter, softened
25 g Cheddar cheese, grated	1 oz Cheddar cheese, grated

Put the broccoli into a pan of boiling salted water, and cook for 10 minutes (if using frozen broccoli, follow the cooking instructions on the packet). Drain very thoroughly. Wrap each piece of broccoli in a slice of ham.

Grease an ovenproof dish with a little of the butter. Arrange the ham rolls in a single layer. Pour on the cheese sauce which has been well seasoned with salt and pepper. Mix the breadcrumbs and butter and sprinkle on top. Sprinkle on the grated cheese. Bake in a moderate oven (180°C, 350°F, Gas Mark 4) for 30 minutes until the top is golden brown and bubbling. Serve very hot. Serves 4

Grecian Leeks

This unusual vegetable dish may be served very hot or chilled as a first course, or as a light meal accompanied by wholemeal bread.

METRIC	IMPERIAL
6 large leeks	6 large leeks
150 ml olive oil	¼ pint olive oil
300 ml dry white wine	½ pint dry white wine
150 ml water	¼ pint water
salt and pepper	salt and pepper
3 bay leaves	3 bay leaves
25 g coriander	1 oz coriander

Remove the roots and dark green tops from the leeks. Wash them very thoroughly and cut each leek lengthways into four pieces. Put these into a large frying pan with all the other ingredients. Bring to the boil and then reduce the heat. Simmer until the leeks are tender and the liquid has been reduced by half. Serve very hot or chilled. Serves 4

Braised Carrots

METRIC	IMPERIAL
450 g medium carrots	1 lb medium carrots
300 ml beef stock	½ pint beef stock
salt and pepper	salt and pepper
pinch of dried thyme	pinch of dried thyme
50 g butter	2 oz butter

Scrape the carrots and leave whole. Put into a pan of cold water, bring to the boil and boil for 10 minutes. Drain very thoroughly. Put into a greased ovenproof dish and add the stock, seasoning and thyme. Cut the butter into thin flakes and distribute over the carrots. Cover and cook in a moderately hot oven (190°C, 375°F, Gas Mark 5) for 30 minutes. Serve with beef, lamb or chicken. Serves 4

Below left: Grecian Leeks; below: Braised Carrots

Sweet Things

Rhubarb Betty

METRIC	IMPERIAL
100 g fresh brown breadcrumbs	4 oz fresh brown breadcrumbs
50 g butter	2 oz butter
50 g light soft brown sugar	2 oz light soft brown sugar
450 g rhubarb	1 lb rhubarb
3 tablespoons water	3 tablespoons water
2 tablespoons golden syrup	2 tablespoons golden syrup

Put the breadcrumbs in a bowl and rub in the butter until the crumbs are lightly coated with the fat. Stir in the sugar. Wipe the rhubarb and cut it into 5-cm/2-inch pieces. Grease an ovenproof dish and put in a third of the crumb mixture. Put half the rhubarb on top. Put on another layer of crumbs, then rhubarb and finally the remaining crumbs.

Mix the water and syrup and pour over the top layer of crumbs. Bake in a moderate oven (180°C, 350°F, Gas Mark 4) for 1 hour. Serve hot with cream or custard. Serves 4

Rhubarb Betty

Lemon Sorbet

Lemon Sorbet

A citrus fruit ice looks very attractive if served in the fruit skins, so it is important to cut them very carefully when preparing the sorbet.

METRIC	IMPERIAL
2 teaspoons powdered gelatine	2 teaspoons powdered gelatine
300 ml water	½ pint water
175 g sugar	6 oz sugar
6 lemons	6 lemons
2 egg whites	2 egg whites

Soak the gelatine in 3 tablespoons of the water. Put the remaining water and sugar into a pan. Heat gently until the sugar has dissolved, and then boil for 5 minutes to make a syrup. Stir in the gelatine and leave to cool.

Cut a 'lid' about one-third of the way down each lemon, and scoop out the flesh carefully into a bowl. Strain off the juice to make up 300 ml/½ pint. Grate a little rind from the base of each lemon skin to make 2 teaspoons. Add the rind and juice to the cool syrup. Whisk the egg whites to stiff peaks, and fold into the syrup. Pour into an ice tray and freeze at the lowest setting of the refrigerator for 1½ hours. Beat the ice until mushy and then continue freezing for 1½ hours.

Wash the lemon skins and dry them well. Spoon in the sorbet, leaving the surface raised above the skins. Put the lids on lightly. Wrap in foil if storing in the freezer. Serves 6

Simnel Cake

This cake is now often eaten as an Easter cake, but originally it was made for the fourth Sunday in Lent, known as Mothering Sunday, which was one of the few days when servant girls could visit their mothers and take them a gift of cake. The almond paste balls on top of the cake represent the Disciples without Judas.

METRIC	IMPERIAL
225 g butter	8 oz butter
225 g sugar	8 oz sugar
350 g plain flour	12 oz plain flour
1 teaspoon ground cinnamon	1 teaspoon ground cinnamon
2 teaspoons baking powder	2 teaspoons baking powder
pinch of grated nutmeg	pinch of grated nutmeg
4 eggs	4 eggs
675 g mixed dried fruit	1½ lb mixed dried fruit
100 g mixed candied peel, chopped	4 oz mixed candied peel, chopped
450 g almond paste	1 lb almond paste
2 tablespoons jam	2 tablespoons jam
beaten egg white to glaze	beaten egg white to glaze
castor sugar to sprinkle	castor sugar to sprinkle
50 g icing sugar	2 oz icing sugar
sugar eggs to decorate	sugar eggs to decorate

Simnel Cake

Cream the butter and sugar until very light and fluffy. Sift together the flour, cinnamon, baking powder and nutmeg. Beat the eggs one at a time into the creamed mixture, adding a little of the flour with each one. Fold in the remaining flour and then the dried fruit and peel.

Roll out the almond paste to make two 20-cm/8-inch rounds, and form the trimmings into eleven round balls. Grease a 20-cm/8-inch round cake tin and line the base with greased paper. Put in half the cake mixture.

1 · Cover with one round of almond paste and then add the remaining cake mixture.

Bake in a moderate oven (160°C, 325°F, Gas Mark 3) for 2½ hours. Cool in the tin.

Remove from the tin and brush the top of the cake with jam. Put on the second round of almond paste.

2 · Place the almond paste balls round the edge in a circle.

Brush lightly with a little egg white and sprinkle with a little castor sugar. Put under a hot grill just long enough for the sugar to turn light brown. Allow to cool completely and mix the icing sugar with enough water to make a smooth icing.

3 · Make a circle of icing in the centre of the cake and arrange the sugar eggs on this.

If liked, add some fluffy chickens, and tie a ribbon or frill around the cake. The icing may be omitted, and the almond paste topping can then be decorated with fresh flowers, or with sugar or artificial ones.

Sand Cake

Sand Cake

This is a light plain cake which is very good with coffee or tea, or it may be served with an ice or fruit.

METRIC	IMPERIAL
50 g butter	2 oz butter
100 g castor sugar	4 oz castor sugar
25 g ground almonds	1 oz ground almonds
2 eggs	2 eggs
25 g plain flour	1 oz plain flour
50 g cornflour	2 oz cornflour
1 teaspoon baking powder	1 teaspoon baking powder
pinch of salt	pinch of salt
2 teaspoons brandy or rum	2 teaspoons brandy or rum
icing sugar to dust	icing sugar to dust

Cream the butter and sugar until very light and white. Stir in the ground almonds, mixing well. Add the eggs separately, beating well between each addition. Sift together the flour, cornflour, baking powder and salt. Fold into the mixture, and then stir in the brandy or rum.

Grease a 0·5-kg/1-lb loaf tin and line the base with greased paper. Spread the mixture evenly in the tin and bake in a moderately hot oven (190°C, 375°F, Gas Mark 5) for 35 minutes. Leave in the tin for 5 minutes, then turn out on a wire rack to cool. When cold, dust the top thickly with sifted icing sugar if liked.

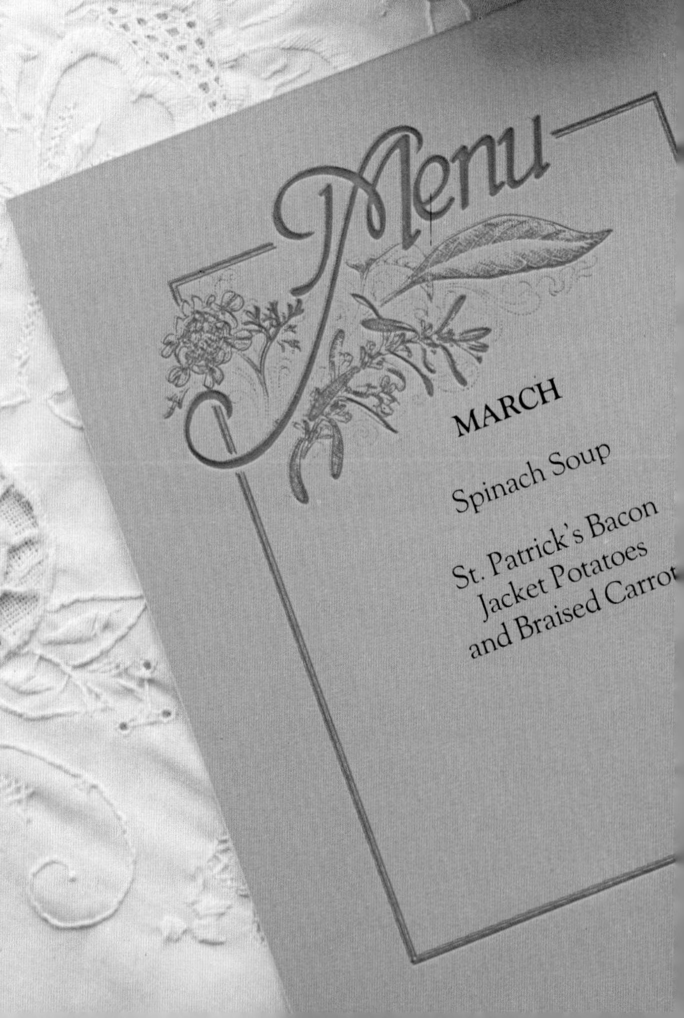

Preserves

Lemon Curd

METRIC	IMPERIAL
4 large lemons	4 large lemons
175 g butter	6 oz butter
450 g sugar	1 lb sugar
4 eggs	4 eggs

Grate the lemon rinds finely, without any of the white pith. Squeeze the juice from the lemons, and strain it into a bowl. Put the butter in the top of a double saucepan, or in a bowl over a pan of hot water. Heat over a low heat until the butter has melted. Add the lemon rind and juice and the sugar.

Beat the eggs well to mix the yolks and whites. Add to the bowl. Heat and stir for about 25 minutes until the mixture is smooth and thick. Pour into hot jars and cover. Lemon curd will keep for 2 months in a cool, dry place. For longer storage, pack in rigid containers and freeze for up to 6 months.

Orange Curd with Candied Peel

METRIC	IMPERIAL
1 large orange	1 large orange
100 g butter	4 oz butter
100 g sugar	4 oz sugar
3 egg yolks	3 egg yolks
50 g candied orange peel, chopped	2 oz candied orange peel, chopped

Grate the orange rind finely and squeeze out the juice. Strain the juice into a bowl. Put the butter and sugar into the top of a double saucepan, or in a bowl over a pan of hot water. Heat until the butter and sugar have melted. Add the orange juice and rind, and the beaten egg yolks. Heat and stir for 5 minutes. Stir in the orange peel and continue heating and stirring for about 15 minutes until thick and creamy.

Pour into hot jars and cover. Orange curd will keep for 2 months in a cool, dry place, or may be frozen. It makes a delicious filling for tarts and cakes.

Orange Curd with Candied Peel

Lemon Curd

April

Easter is
the time for eggs
and poultry and for
little gifts for the family.
Make the best of eggs for lighter
meals and delicious puddings, and encourage the
children to make sweets for presents.
Try a very special dish of
duck or lamb during
the Easter
weekend.

Foods in Season

FISH
Brill · Crab · Crayfish · Lobster · Mackerel · Oysters · Plaice · Prawns · Salmon
Salmon trout · Trout · Turbot · Whitebait

POULTRY AND GAME
Chicken · Duck · Goose · Guinea fowl · Turkey

VEGETABLES
(home produced and imported)
Broccoli · Chicory · Leeks · Parsnips · Spinach

FRUIT
(home produced and imported)
Grapefruit · Lemons · Oranges · Pineapple · Rhubarb

Freezer Notes

There will be more lamb available for freezing, and those who like seafood such as crabs and prawns may like to freeze some now. As well as broccoli, there is now spinach in good supply in the garden. This is also a month to find small pineapples in the shops which freeze very well in sugared slices. As the weather improves, this is a good time to put extra bread, pies and cakes in the freezer ready for outdoor picnics and expeditions.

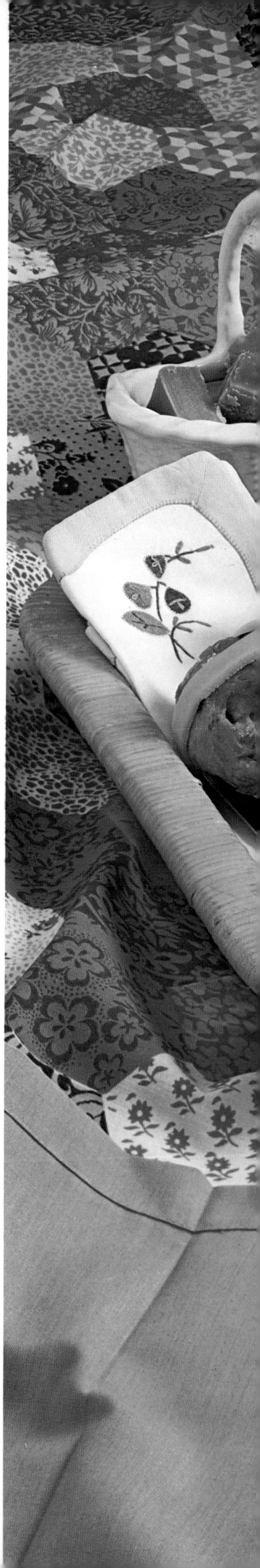

HAPPY
EASTER

Starters

Eggs in Tarragon Aspic

Eggs set in lightly herb-flavoured aspic make a delicious first course, or a light meal with salad. Egg-shaped moulds may be found in specialist shops, or the eggs may be set in individual ramekins. The aspic is most easily prepared from packet crystals.

METRIC	IMPERIAL
4 eggs	4 eggs
4 thin slices cooked ham	4 thin slices cooked ham
4 sprigs tarragon	4 sprigs tarragon
300 ml aspic	½ pint aspic

Put the eggs into a pan of cold water. Bring to the boil and boil for exactly 8 minutes. Cover the eggs with cold water immediately. As soon as they are cold, peel the eggs carefully. Trim all fat from the ham slices, which must be paper thin. Make up the aspic and cool until syrupy.

Put a tablespoon of aspic into each of four ramekins or egg-shaped moulds. Place a small sprig of tarragon in each one. Leave in the refrigerator for a few minutes until set firmly. Wrap each egg in a piece of ham to enclose it completely. Put a wrapped egg into each container with the joins of the ham on top. Pour in the remaining aspic to fill the containers. Chill until firm. Trim any ends of ham which are sticking above the rim of the containers. Turn out the eggs carefully on to a serving dish. Garnish with lettuce or watercress if liked. Serves 4

Fish and Tomato Lasagne

Although this dish is usually served as a starter, it makes a delicious luncheon or supper dish. Serve with hot French bread or a salad.

METRIC	IMPERIAL
350 g haddock fillets	12 oz haddock fillets
175 g lasagne	6 oz lasagne
300 ml cheese sauce	½ pint cheese sauce
2 green peppers, chopped	2 green peppers, chopped
1 small onion, chopped	1 small onion, chopped
2 tablespoons oil	2 tablespoons oil
4 large tomatoes, peeled	4 large tomatoes, peeled
salt and pepper	salt and pepper
100 g Cheddar cheese, grated	4 oz Cheddar cheese, grated

Fish and Tomato Lasagne

Eggs in Tarragon Aspic

Skin the fish and cut it into 2·5-cm/1-inch pieces. Put half the fish into a greased shallow ovenproof dish. Cover with half the sheets of lasagne and half the cheese sauce. Put the peppers and onion into a small pan with the oil. Remove the seeds from the tomatoes and chop the flesh. Cook the peppers and onions until soft but not coloured. Stir in the pieces of tomato and continue cooking for 5 minutes.

Spread half this mixture on the cheese sauce and season well. Top with the remaining fish and lasagne. Add the remaining tomato mixture and finally the cheese sauce. Sprinkle cheese on top. Cook in a moderately hot oven (190°C, 375°F, Gas Mark 5) for 50 minutes, and serve hot. It is not necessary to cook the sheets of lasagne before making up the dish as it cooks very well in the sauce in the oven. Serves 4

Smoked Haddock Omelette

This omelette has a topping of creamy smoked haddock, and should not be folded over. The topping has to be lightly browned under the grill, and the omelette is then served in wedges. This dish is also suitable to serve for a light luncheon or as a supper dish. Serve with a salad or a green vegetable such as spinach.

METRIC	IMPERIAL
6 eggs	6 eggs
salt and pepper	salt and pepper
25 g butter	1 oz butter
Topping	*Topping*
225 g smoked haddock, cooked	8 oz smoked haddock, cooked
300 ml cheese sauce	½ pint cheese sauce
3 tablespoons double cream	3 tablespoons double cream
50 g cheese, grated	2 oz cheese, grated

Prepare the topping before making the omelette. Flake the haddock and mix into the cheese sauce. Stir in the cream. Heat this mixture gently, stirring well.

Break the eggs into a bowl and break them up lightly with a fork. Season with salt and pepper. Melt the butter in a large omelette pan, and pour in the eggs. Cook and stir with a fork until the base of the omelette is golden brown and the top is just set. Take off the heat and quickly spread with the fish mixture. Sprinkle with grated cheese and put under a hot grill until the cheese has just changed colour. Serve at once. Serves 4

Smoked Haddock Omelette

Main Dishes

Seafood Pie

METRIC	IMPERIAL
450 g cod fillet, cooked	1 lb cod fillet, cooked
100 g peeled prawns	4 oz peeled prawns
2 eggs, hard-boiled and chopped	2 eggs, hard-boiled and chopped
100 g button mushrooms	4 oz button mushrooms
25 g butter	1 oz butter
100 g shelled peas	4 oz shelled peas
1 egg	1 egg
300 ml white sauce	½ pint white sauce
1 tablespoon chopped parsley	1 tablespoon chopped parsley
salt and pepper	salt and pepper
450 g mashed potato	1 lb mashed potato
25 g cheese, grated	1 oz cheese, grated

Flake the fish and put into a 1-litre/2-pint pie dish. Mix with the prawns and chopped eggs. Cook the whole mushrooms in the butter until just tender. Add to the fish. If the peas are frozen, add them uncooked; otherwise cook the peas in boiling water for 10 minutes, drain and add to the fish.

Beat the egg and white sauce together and stir in the parsley and seasoning. Mix into the fish so that the ingredients are well covered with sauce. Top with the mashed potato, using a piping bag and star nozzle to pipe a trellis pattern for an attractive finish. Sprinkle with cheese. Bake in a moderate oven (180°C, 350°F, Gas Mark 4) for 30 minutes. Serves 4–6

Guard of Honour with Apricot Stuffing

Guard of Honour with Apricot Stuffing

A 'guard of honour' is made with two best ends of neck of lamb which are chined and arranged so that the ends of the bones rest on each other like the swords of a guard of honour. This attractive joint can be prepared by a butcher with due notice, but it is not difficult to prepare at home.

METRIC	IMPERIAL
2 best ends of neck of lamb, chined	2 best ends of neck of lamb, chined
100 g canned apricots	4 oz canned apricots
100 g fresh breadcrumbs	4 oz fresh breadcrumbs
grated rind of 1 lemon	grated rind of 1 lemon
2 teaspoons dried thyme	2 teaspoons dried thyme
2 teaspoons chopped parsley	2 teaspoons chopped parsley
salt and pepper	salt and pepper
1 egg	1 egg
watercress to garnish	watercress to garnish

Trim the fat and skin from the ends of the bones to leave 2·5 cms/1 inch bone protruding. Put the two joints facing each other in a roasting tin, so that the tips cross and interlace. Cover the bone tips with foil.

Drain and chop the apricots finely and mix with the breadcrumbs, lemon rind, thyme, parsley, seasoning and egg. Add a little of the apricot syrup to bind the stuffing, but keep it slightly crumbly. Form into balls the size of walnuts. Roast the meat in a moderate oven (180°C, 350°F, Gas Mark 4) for 45 minutes. Arrange the stuffing around the meat and continue cooking for 30 minutes. Serve the meat with the stuffing balls, garnished with watercress. Serves 6

Chicken in Lemon Sauce

This is a useful springtime dish as it may be served hot or cold, and it is particularly attractive as part of a buffet meal.

METRIC	IMPERIAL
675 g cooked chicken	1½ lb cooked chicken
1 lemon	1 lemon
300 ml white sauce, cooled	½ pint white sauce, cooled
salt and pepper	salt and pepper
300 ml double cream	½ pint double cream
450 g boiled rice	1 lb boiled rice
paprika	paprika

If the chicken is boiled, some of the stock may be used to make the white sauce. Cut the chicken meat in neat slices. Remove the peel from the lemon and cut it in thin shreds. Simmer the shreds in a little boiling water for 3 minutes. Drain and reserve the shreds. Squeeze the juice from the lemon and add it to the white sauce. Season and stir in the cream.

Arrange a bed of rice on a serving dish. Put the chicken slices neatly in the centre. Coat the chicken with the sauce and sprinkle with paprika. Sprinkle the reserved lemon shreds on the rice.

To serve the dish hot, use hot rice and put the chicken slices on top. Heat the sauce gently and pour over the chicken. Cover with foil and heat in a moderate oven (160°C, 325°F, Gas Mark 3) for 20 minutes. Sprinkle with paprika and lemon shreds as for the cold dish. Serves 4–6

Duck with Cherries

METRIC	IMPERIAL
1 (1·75-kg) duck	1 (4-lb) duck
225 g canned black cherries, drained and stoned	8 oz canned black cherries, drained and stoned
150 ml stock	¼ pint stock
1 wineglass dry sherry	1 wineglass dry sherry
salt and pepper	salt and pepper
2 teaspoons cherry brandy	2 teaspoons cherry brandy

Prick the duck with a fork and season it well inside and out with salt and pepper. Roast in a moderate oven (180°C, 350°F, Gas Mark 4) for 20 minutes. Strain off the fat and continue cooking for 1 hour. Drain off any surplus fat. Put the duck on a serving dish and keep warm.

Put the cherries, stock and sherry into the roasting tin and heat gently, stirring well. Season to taste and simmer until the cherries are very tender. Remove from the heat, stir in the cherry brandy and pour over the duck. If possible, serve with new potatoes and peas. For easier serving the duck may be carved beforehand and arranged in slices with the cherries. Serves 4–5

Below left: Chicken in Lemon Sauce; below right: Duck with Cherries

Coffee Mousse

Sweet Things

Coffee Mousse

METRIC	IMPERIAL
3 eggs, separated	3 eggs, separated
75 g castor sugar	3 oz castor sugar
300 ml strong black coffee	½ pint strong black coffee
15 g powdered gelatine	½ oz powdered gelatine
300 ml double cream	½ pint double cream
Decoration	*Decoration*
150 ml double cream	¼ pint double cream
50 g walnuts, chopped	2 oz walnuts, chopped
25 g plain chocolate	1 oz plain chocolate

Prepare a 600-ml/1-pint soufflé dish by tying a band of double kitchen foil around the outside of the dish, to stand 5 cm/2 inches above the rim. Put the egg yolks, sugar and half the coffee into a bowl over a pan of hot water. Heat gently and whisk until the mixture is thick enough to coat the back of a spoon. Put the remaining coffee in a small pan with the gelatine and heat gently until the gelatine has dissolved. Stir into the egg mixture and leave until cool and beginning to thicken.

Whip the cream to soft peaks. In another bowl, whisk the egg whites to stiff peaks. Fold the cream into the egg mixture, and then fold in the egg whites. Spoon into the dish and chill until firm. Use a wide-bladed knife dipped in water to ease away the foil, and remove, leaving the set mixture standing above the dish. Coat the sides with chopped walnuts. Whip the cream and pipe in rosettes around the edge of the mousse. Grate the chocolate coarsely and sprinkle on to the cream. Serves 6

Chocolate Meringue Pie

This is a rich pudding for those who love chocolate, and it needs very little cooking time.

METRIC	IMPERIAL
50 g butter	2 oz butter
50 g sugar	2 oz sugar
1 tablespoon golden syrup	1 tablespoon golden syrup
175 g chocolate digestive biscuits	6 oz chocolate digestive biscuits
175 g plain chocolate	6 oz plain chocolate
3 eggs	3 eggs
2 teaspoons brandy	2 teaspoons brandy
150 ml double cream	¼ pint double cream
Topping	*Topping*
2 egg whites	2 egg whites
100 g castor sugar	4 oz castor sugar

Rhubarb Compote

Early pink rhubarb is very good cooked this way without any water. This mixture freezes very well.

METRIC	IMPERIAL
450 g rhubarb	1 lb rhubarb
175 g marmalade	6 oz marmalade
25 g light soft brown sugar	1 oz light soft brown sugar
¼ teaspoon ground ginger	¼ teaspoon ground ginger

Wash the rhubarb and cut it into 5-cm/2-inch pieces. Put into a pan with the marmalade, sugar and ginger, and cook over low heat, stirring occasionally until the fruit is soft but not broken. Pour into a serving bowl or individual dishes and chill. Serve with small sweet biscuits. The flavour may be varied by using dark chunky marmalade, jelly marmalade or lemon marmalade according to taste. Serves 4–6

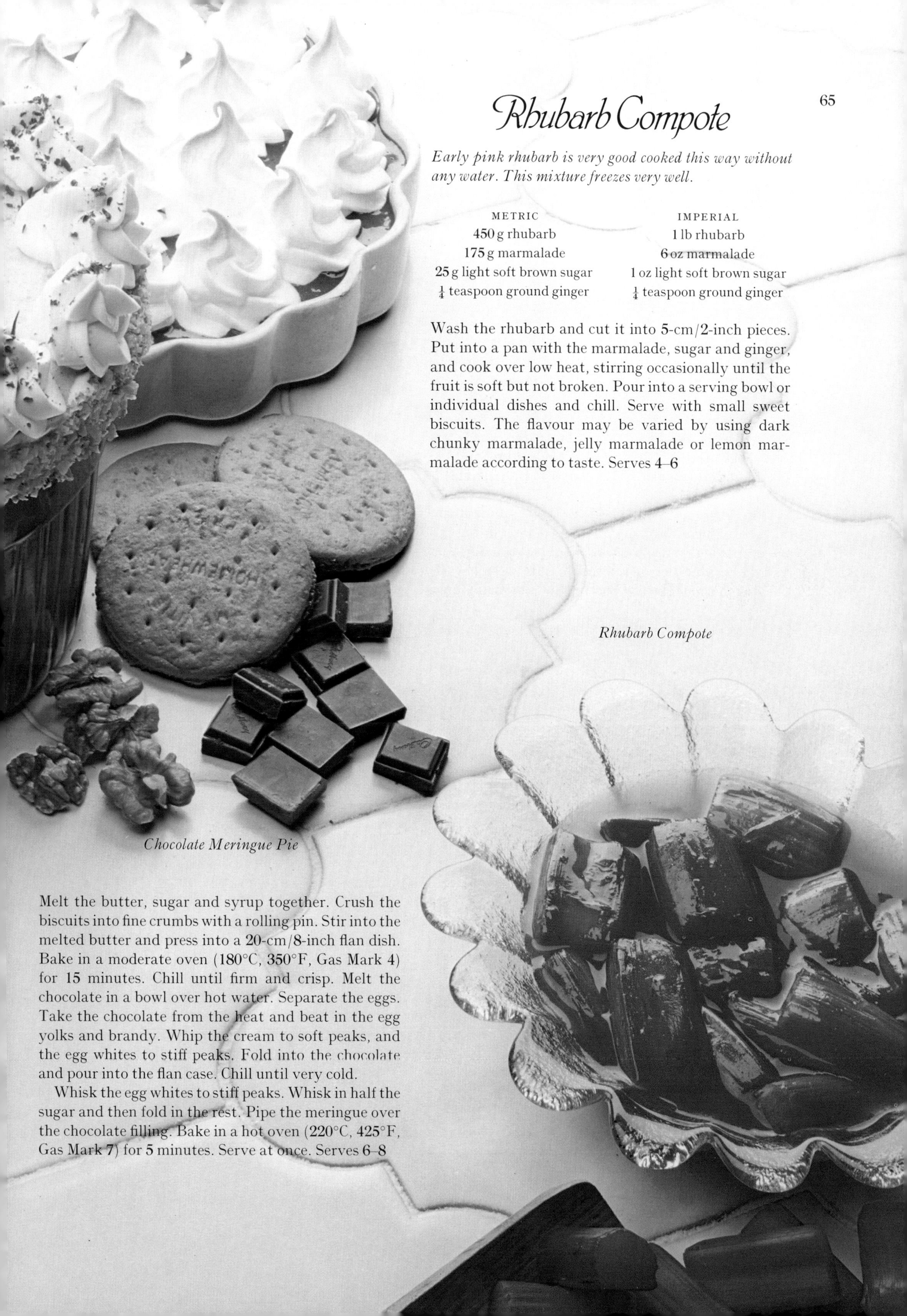

Rhubarb Compote

Chocolate Meringue Pie

Melt the butter, sugar and syrup together. Crush the biscuits into fine crumbs with a rolling pin. Stir into the melted butter and press into a 20-cm/8-inch flan dish. Bake in a moderate oven (180°C, 350°F, Gas Mark 4) for 15 minutes. Chill until firm and crisp. Melt the chocolate in a bowl over hot water. Separate the eggs. Take the chocolate from the heat and beat in the egg yolks and brandy. Whip the cream to soft peaks, and the egg whites to stiff peaks. Fold into the chocolate and pour into the flan case. Chill until very cold.

Whisk the egg whites to stiff peaks. Whisk in half the sugar and then fold in the rest. Pipe the meringue over the chocolate filling. Bake in a hot oven (220°C, 425°F, Gas Mark 7) for 5 minutes. Serve at once. Serves 6–8

Easter Treats

Easter Biscuits

METRIC	IMPERIAL
225 g plain flour	8 oz plain flour
pinch of salt	pinch of salt
½ teaspoon ground mixed spice	½ teaspoon ground mixed spice
75 g butter	3 oz butter
75 g castor sugar	3 oz castor sugar
1 egg	1 egg
75 g currants	3 oz currants
grated rind of ½ lemon	grated rind of ½ lemon
2 teaspoons brandy	2 teaspoons brandy
milk to brush	milk to brush
castor sugar to sprinkle	castor sugar to sprinkle

Sift the flour, salt and spice into a bowl. Cream the butter and sugar until light and fluffy. Beat in the egg and a little flour, and then work in the remaining flour. Add the currants, lemon rind and brandy and mix well. The dough should be like pastry. Roll out thinly on a lightly floured board, and cut into large rounds using the top of a glass or round pastry cutter.

Arrange on a greased baking tray and prick four or five times with a fork. Brush over with a little milk and sprinkle with a little extra castor sugar. Bake in a moderate oven (160°C, 325°F, Gas Mark 3) for 20 minutes. The biscuits should be very pale gold in colour. Lift carefully on to a wire rack to cool. Store in an airtight container, packing carefully to prevent breakages.

Hot Cross Buns

METRIC	IMPERIAL
450 g strong plain flour	1 lb strong plain flour
300 ml milk and water, mixed	½ pint milk and water, mixed
15 g fresh yeast	½ oz fresh yeast
pinch of salt	pinch of salt
1 teaspoon ground cinnamon	1 teaspoon ground cinnamon
1 teaspoon grated nutmeg	1 teaspoon grated nutmeg
50 g castor sugar	2 oz castor sugar
75 g currants	3 oz currants
25 g mixed candied peel, chopped	1 oz mixed candied peel, chopped
50 g butter	2 oz butter
1 egg	1 egg
sugar and milk to glaze	sugar and milk to glaze

Put half the flour into a warm bowl. Heat the milk and water to lukewarm. Mix the yeast with a little of the liquid and then add the remaining liquid. Pour into the bowl and mix well with the flour. Cover with a damp cloth and leave in a warm place for 40 minutes.

Mix together the remaining flour, salt, cinnamon, nutmeg and sugar, and stir in the currants and peel. Warm the butter until just melted. Break up the egg with a fork. Add all the dry ingredients to the yeast mixture and pour in the butter and egg. Mix thoroughly with the hands or with the dough hook on a mixer. Return to a clean greased bowl, cover with a damp cloth and leave in a warm place for 1 hour.

Divide the dough into 16 pieces, and shape each piece into a bun. Put on a greased and floured baking tray, leaving room for the buns to spread. Make a cross on each bun using a knife (or put on a cross made from narrow strips of shortcrust pastry). Cover and leave in a warm place for 40 minutes.

Bake in a hot oven (220°C, 425°F, Gas Mark 7) for 15 minutes. Meanwhile, dissolve 3 tablespoons sugar in 3 tablespoons milk over low heat. Brush this glaze over the buns with a pastry brush, and return to the oven for 5 minutes more cooking. Cool on a wire rack.

Russian Easter Bread; Hot Cross Buns

Russian Easter Bread

METRIC	IMPERIAL
150 ml milk	¼ pint milk
25 g fresh yeast	1 oz fresh yeast
225 g strong plain flour	8 oz strong plain flour
3 egg yolks	3 egg yolks
pinch of salt	pinch of salt
75 g butter, melted	3 oz butter, melted
75 g sugar	3 oz sugar
100 g mixed candied peel, chopped	4 oz mixed candied peel, chopped
egg and milk to glaze	egg and milk to glaze

Heat the milk to lukewarm and stir in the yeast. Add 25 g/1 oz of the flour and leave in a warm place covered with a cloth for 30 minutes. In another bowl, beat the egg yolks, salt, butter and sugar together. Mix in the yeast mixture and the remaining flour to give a soft dough. Stir in the peel. Cover with a damp cloth and leave to rise in a warm place for 1½ hours.

Divide the mixture into three pieces and plait them loosely. Put on to a floured baking tray and cover with a damp cloth. Leave to stand in a warm place for 30 minutes. Mix a little beaten egg and milk together and brush over the surface of the bread. Bake in a moderately hot oven (200°C, 400°F, Gas Mark 6) for 40 minutes. Put on a wire rack to cool.

Decorated Easter Eggs

An egg makes a good breakfast on Easter Sunday, and the family will enjoy being given specially decorated ones. Coloured eggs can be drawn on to give pretty patterns, names, initials or funny faces.

If liked, plain, cooked eggs can be used for decorating, but a more unusual effect is obtained by colouring the eggs all over. Put the eggs to be coloured in a bowl and cover them with vinegar. Leave for 30 minutes then drain. Add vegetable colouring of your choice to the cooking water and cook the eggs. If the eggs are to be eaten for breakfast, soft-boil them for about 4 minutes. For a picnic, hard-boil the eggs for 10 minutes and immerse them in cold water at once to prevent a dark ring from forming around the yolk.

Rest the cooked eggs in an egg cup to draw on the design. In this way the egg is held firmly, there is no danger of smudging the finished egg, and only the area which will show is decorated. Draw or write on the eggs with a felt-tipped pen, and if the eggs are to be eaten hot, serve them immediately.

Use individual saucepans of coloured water to boil the eggs if you want to serve a bowl of differently coloured eggs.

Easter Chocolate Nests

Easter Chocolate Nests

These little chocolate nests filled with miniature eggs will be very popular with the children, who can easily make them for teatime on Easter Sunday.

METRIC	IMPERIAL
50 g butter	2 oz butter
2 tablespoons golden syrup	2 tablespoons golden syrup
25 g cocoa	1 oz cocoa
50 g castor sugar	2 oz castor sugar
50 g crispy rice cereal	2 oz crispy rice cereal
sugar eggs	sugar eggs

Put the butter and syrup into a large pan and heat until just melted. Remove from the heat and stir in the cocoa until well mixed. Add the sugar and cereal and stir until completely coated. Grease a baking tray very lightly and spoon on 12 heaps of the mixture. Hollow the centres lightly with a teaspoon. Leave until cold and set. Lift off the baking tray very carefully with a palette knife, and put on to a plate. Put three or four small coloured sugar eggs into each nest.

Decorated Easter Eggs

Honey Fudge

METRIC	IMPERIAL
225 g honey	8 oz honey
900 g granulated sugar	2 lb granulated sugar
100 g butter	4 oz butter
1 (225-g) can sweetened condensed milk	1 (8 oz) can sweetened condensed milk
150 ml milk	¼ pint milk

Put all the ingredients together in a large thick pan and stir well. Bring to the boil, then heat to 114°C/237°F (when a little dropped into a cup of cold water will form into a soft ball). Take off the heat and beat hard with a wooden spoon until the mixture is thick and creamy. Pour into a greased tin and cut into squares when cold.

Honey Fudge

May

Warmer weather brings the first early vegetables and fruit – gooseberries used to be a traditional Whitsun dish. The days may even be warm enough for some cool outdoor meals, using tiny new vegetables, salads and fresh herbs, and finishing with a refreshing home-made fruit ice.

Foods in Season

FISH

Brill · Crab · Crayfish · Haddock · Herring · Lobster · Mullet · Plaice · Prawns · Salmon
Salmon trout · Sole · Trout · Turbot · Whitebait

POULTRY AND GAME

Chicken · Duck · Guinea fowl

VEGETABLES
(home produced and imported)

Asparagus · Broad beans · Broccoli · Carrots · Cauliflower · Courgettes · Globe artichokes
Peas · Spinach

FRUIT
(home produced and imported)

Apricots · Gooseberries · Lemons · Oranges · Pineapple · Rhubarb

Freezer Notes

Early vegetables begin to flood in, and there is plenty of choice for stocking the freezer. Early asparagus, broad beans, broccoli, carrots, peas and spinach all freeze very well and give plenty of variety to meals. Many fish are in season and may be brought back from seaside trips for speedy preparation for the freezer.

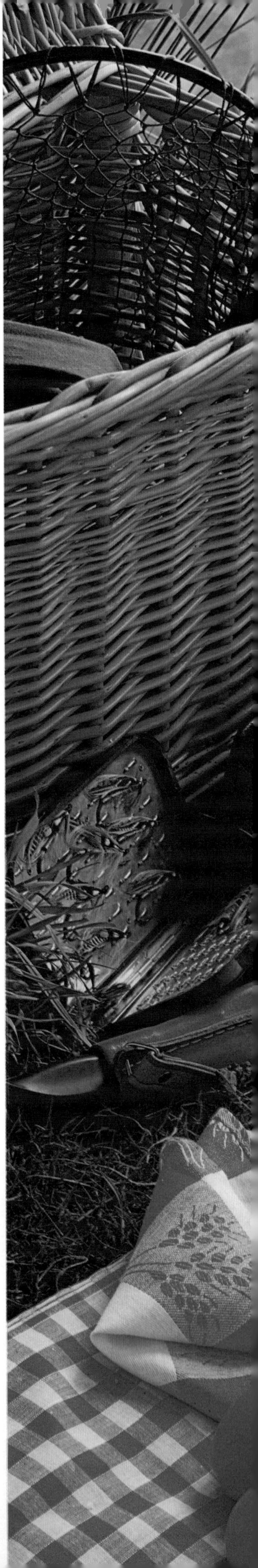

Starters

Italian Asparagus

Serve asparagus as a first course, or as a light meal with thin brown bread and butter. If fresh asparagus is not available, use the frozen variety. Asparagus can also be served with Hollandaise sauce (see page 75).

METRIC	IMPERIAL
900 g asparagus	2 lb asparagus
4 tablespoons olive oil	4 tablespoons olive oil
2 cloves garlic, crushed	2 cloves garlic, crushed
salt and pepper	salt and pepper
2 teaspoons lemon juice	2 teaspoons lemon juice
40 g grated Parmesan cheese	1½ oz grated Parmesan cheese

Tie the asparagus in four bundles. Stand upright in a pan of boiling salted water, cover and cook for about 15 minutes until the stems are tender. The water in the pan should come about two-thirds of the way up the stems so that the lower part of the asparagus is boiled while the delicate tips are steamed. Drain very thoroughly, untie the bundles and arrange on a warm serving dish.

Heat the oil with the garlic, until the garlic is just golden. Remove from the heat and stir in the salt, pepper and lemon juice. Pour over the asparagus and sprinkle with cheese. Serve at once. Serves 4

Avocado Mousse

METRIC	IMPERIAL
300 ml mayonnaise	½ pint mayonnaise
300 ml double cream	½ pint double cream
3 avocados	3 avocados
2 teaspoons lemon juice	2 teaspoons lemon juice
3 drops of Tabasco sauce	3 drops of Tabasco sauce
½ teaspoon Worcestershire sauce	½ teaspoon Worcestershire sauce
15 g gelatine	½ oz gelatine

Put the mayonnaise in a bowl. Whip the cream to soft peaks and blend well with the mayonnaise. Scoop the avocado flesh out of the skins and mash thoroughly with the lemon juice, Tabasco and Worcestershire sauces. Fold into the cream mixture. Put the gelatine into a cup with 2 tablespoons water and stand the cup in a pan of hot water until the gelatine becomes syrupy. Cool the gelatine and fold into the cream mixture. Pour into an oiled mould and chill, or pour into six individual ramekins. If liked, garnish with thinly sliced cucumber. Serves 6

Below left: Italian Asparagus; below: Avocado Mousse; far right: Potted Crabmeat

Potted Crabmeat

METRIC	IMPERIAL
225 g crabmeat	8 oz crabmeat
100 g butter	4 oz butter
1 teaspoon ground black pepper	1 teaspoon ground black pepper
1 teaspoon ground mace	1 teaspoon ground mace
pinch of cayenne pepper	pinch of cayenne pepper
juice of ½ lemon	juice of ½ lemon

The crabmeat may be fresh, canned or frozen. Break it up into shreds with a fork. Melt 25 g/1 oz of the butter in a pan and stir in the pepper, mace and cayenne. Add the crab and lemon juice and stir over low heat until the crabmeat is hot but not brown. Put into small pots. Heat the remaining butter until foamy, skim, and pour over the crabmeat to cover it completely. Chill until firm. Serve with toast and wedges of lemon. Serves 4

Main Dishes

Baked Salmon

If salmon is baked in foil, it remains full of flavour and very moist. It is worth cooking a large piece as cold salmon is so good with a salad. The tail-end is sometimes a little cheaper and some people say it has a better flavour. Small new potatoes and green peas are traditional accompaniments for salmon, together with hollandaise sauce and cucumber salad.

METRIC	IMPERIAL
1·75 kg salmon	4 lb salmon
2 large sprigs fennel or dill	2 large sprigs fennel or dill
1 lemon	1 lemon
salt and pepper	salt and pepper
100 g butter	4 oz butter

1 · Grease a large piece of kitchen foil and put the salmon in the centre. Insert the fennel or dill in the centre of the salmon. Cut the lemon in half, and cut one half in thin slices. Insert these in the centre of the salmon.

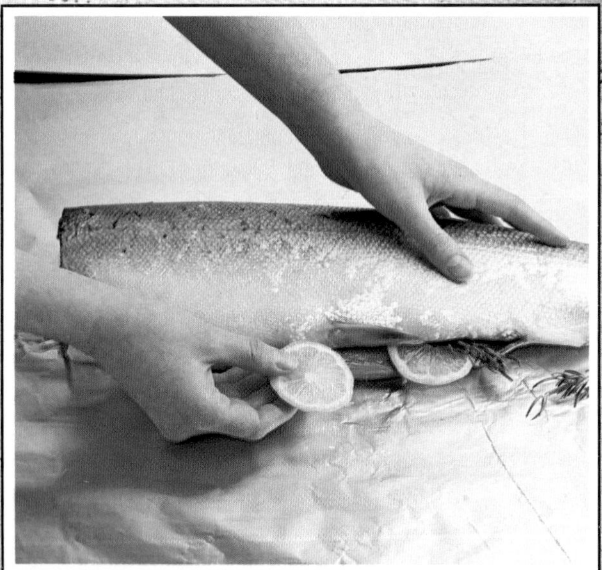

Squeeze the remaining half over the salmon on both sides. Sprinkle the inside of the fish with salt and pepper, and salt and pepper the skin on both sides. Cut the butter in flakes and put a quarter inside the salmon. Dot the remaining butter on top of the fish. Fold over the foil to make a secure parcel. Put on a baking tray and bake in a moderately hot oven (200°C, 400°F, Gas Mark 6) for 1 hour. Unwrap the salmon.

Cucumber Salad

2 · Remove the skin and lemon and fennel before serving with peas and new potatoes.

If plenty of fennel or dill is available, use more to garnish the fish. Serves 8

Baked Salmon;
above: Hollandaise Sauce

Hollandaise Sauce

This is a simple way of making a rather special sauce which is the perfect accompaniment to salmon, and also to globe artichokes and asparagus.

METRIC	IMPERIAL
1½ tablespoons lemon juice	1½ tablespoons lemon juice
1 tablespoon cold water	1 tablespoon cold water
1 egg yolk	1 egg yolk
salt and white pepper	salt and white pepper
125 g unsalted butter	5 oz unsalted butter

Make this sauce in a bowl over a pan of hot water. The water must be kept hot, but not boiling, as it will spoil the sauce if it splashes into the mixture. Before beginning the recipe, make sure the butter is soft, but not melted. Put the lemon juice, water, egg yolk, seasoning and a third of the butter into the bowl. Beat with a hand whisk until the butter has melted. Add the remaining butter a teaspoon at a time, beating until the sauce thickens like mayonnaise. Serve at once. Serves 4

Cucumber Salad

METRIC	IMPERIAL
1 cucumber	1 cucumber
150 ml white vinegar	¼ pint white vinegar
150 ml water	¼ pint water
salt and white pepper	salt and white pepper
1 teaspoon sugar	1 teaspoon sugar
1 tablespoon chopped parsley to garnish	1 tablespoon chopped parsley to garnish

Peel the cucumber and cut it in very thin slices. Put into a bowl and cover with the vinegar, water, salt, pepper and sugar. Leave in a cold place for 2 hours. Drain very well. Sprinkle with chopped parsley. Serves 4–6

Salmon in a Parcel

This is a delicious way of using cold salmon, but smoked haddock may be used instead, or even cold chicken.

METRIC	IMPERIAL
450 g frozen puff pastry	1 lb frozen puff pastry
350 g cooked salmon	12 oz cooked salmon
175 g cooked rice	6 oz cooked rice
3 eggs, hard-boiled and chopped	3 eggs, hard-boiled and chopped
50 g cooked peas	2 oz cooked peas
50 g button mushrooms	2 oz button mushrooms
25 g butter	1 oz butter
8 tablespoons water	8 tablespoons water
1 tablespoon chopped parsley	1 tablespoon chopped parsley
few drops of Tabasco sauce	few drops of Tabasco sauce
salt and pepper	salt and pepper
beaten egg to glaze	beaten egg to glaze

Roll out the pastry evenly into a rectangle 30 × 38 cm/12 × 15 inches. Flake the fish and mix well with the rice, eggs and peas. Cook the whole mushrooms in the butter until just tender. Add the remaining ingredients and the fish mixture and stir over a gentle heat until hot. Cool slightly and place down the centre of the pastry. Fold over the sides and ends and seal firmly. Cut three diagonal slashes on the top, and brush with beaten egg to glaze. Put on a baking tray and bake in a hot oven (220°C, 425°F, Gas Mark 7) for 40 minutes, until crisp and golden. Serve hot with parsley sauce, or cold with salad. Serves 6

Mackerel with Gooseberry Sauce

METRIC	IMPERIAL
4 mackerel	4 mackerel
15 g seasoned flour	½ oz seasoned flour
Sauce	*Sauce*
25 g butter	1 oz butter
25 g plain flour	1 oz plain flour
225 g green gooseberries	8 oz green gooseberries
salt and pepper	salt and pepper
pinch of sugar	pinch of sugar

Clean, gut and wash the mackerel and remove the heads. Make two slanting incisions with a sharp knife across both sides of each fish. Dust the fish lightly with the seasoned flour. Remove the rack from the grill pan and oil the pan lightly. Grill the fish for about 8 minutes each side under medium heat.

While the fish is cooking, prepare the sauce. Melt the butter and stir in the flour. Cook for 2 minutes. Stir in 475 ml/¾ pint water to make a smooth thin sauce. Top and tail the gooseberries and add them to the sauce. Add salt, pepper and sugar and simmer until the berries are soft. Put through a sieve, reheat and serve very hot with the fish. Serves 4

Left: Salmon in a Parcel; right: Mackerel with Gooseberry Sauce

GINGER

Lamb in Mint Jelly

Cold left-over lamb is not always popular, but this recipe transforms it into a delicious dish which is suitable for a buffet party on a warm day. The lamb is nicest if slightly pink and juicy.

METRIC	IMPERIAL
450 g cooked lamb from the leg	1 lb cooked lamb from the leg
300 ml aspic jelly	½ pint aspic jelly
2 tablespoons dry sherry	2 tablespoons dry sherry
2 tablespoons chopped fresh mint	2 tablespoons chopped fresh mint
8 medium tomatoes	8 medium tomatoes
225 g cooked peas	8 oz cooked peas

Cut the lamb in neat slices and arrange on a serving dish. Make up the aspic and leave until cool and syrupy. Stir in the sherry and mint and spoon about two-thirds of the jelly over the lamb to cover it completely.

Peel the tomatoes and cut a small lid from the top of each one. Scoop out the seeds and drain off any liquid. Fill each tomato with peas so that they come above the surface. Spoon over the remaining aspic and arrange the tomatoes round the lamb. Chill before serving with a green salad. Serves 4

Boiled Bacon with Parsley Sauce

Boiled bacon is traditionally served accompanied by broad beans and parsley sauce. This is a combination served in country areas, made particularly tasty and attractive if served with boiled carrots as a colourful vegetable.

METRIC	IMPERIAL
1 (1·25-kg) bacon joint	1 (2½-lb) bacon joint
1 small onion	1 small onion
1 medium carrot	1 medium carrot
1 bay leaf	1 bay leaf
1 sprig thyme	1 sprig thyme
1 sprig parsley	1 sprig parsley
4 peppercorns	4 peppercorns
2 teaspoons light soft brown sugar	2 teaspoons light soft brown sugar
450 g broad beans, shelled	1 lb broad beans, shelled
Sauce	*Sauce*
25 g butter	1 oz butter
25 g plain flour	1 oz plain flour
600 ml milk	1 pint milk
4 tablespoons chopped parsley	4 tablespoons chopped parsley

Put the bacon in a pan and cover with cold water. Bring to the boil and drain off the water. Cover with fresh water and add the onion, carrot, bay leaf, thyme, parsley, peppercorns and sugar. Bring to the boil, reduce the heat, cover and simmer for 1¼ hours.

Cook the beans in boiling salted water until just tender (they may be cooked with the bacon for the last 15 minutes if liked).

Melt the butter, work in the flour and cook for 1 minute. Gradually stir in the milk and stir over a low heat until the sauce is smooth and creamy. Season to taste and stir in the parsley. Slice the bacon and arrange on a serving dish. Surround with the beans and pour on a little of the cooking liquid. Serve the sauce separately. Serves 8

Pork Tenderloin in Cream Sauce

The tenderloin is a long thin piece of lean meat which is the equivalent of fillet steak.

METRIC	IMPERIAL
1 pork tenderloin	1 pork tenderloin
25 g butter	1 oz butter
1 tablespoon oil	1 tablespoon oil
1 tablespoon brandy	1 tablespoon brandy
300 ml double cream	½ pint double cream
2 teaspoons chopped parsley to garnish	2 teaspoons chopped parsley to garnish

Use a sharp knife to cut slices from the tenderloin. Cut it downwards and slightly on the bias, and cut as thinly as possible. Put the pieces on a sheet of greaseproof paper, cover with more paper, and beat the pieces out very thinly with a meat hammer or other heavy object.

Heat the butter and oil and cook a few slices of pork at a time very gently until they are just coloured and cooked through. Lift out the cooked meat on to a warm serving dish and keep warm. When all the meat is cooked, pour the brandy into the pan juices and light with a match. As soon as the flame dies down, pour in the cream and stir very gently over low heat until just warmed through. Season to taste. Pour over the pork and sprinkle on the parsley. Serve at once with new potatoes, peas or beans, or with a salad. Serves 4

Left: Pork Tenderloin in Cream Sauce; right: Cold Chicken Curry

Cold Chicken Curry

Cold curry is surprisingly good to eat, and left-over curry may be eaten with a rice salad and chutney. This recipe is for a rather special curry which may be served for a party or other special meal.

METRIC	IMPERIAL
1 (1·5-kg) chicken, cooked	1 (3-lb) chicken, cooked
1 tablespoon oil	1 tablespoon oil
1 medium onion, chopped	1 medium onion, chopped
3 teaspoons curry powder	3 teaspoons curry powder
1 teaspoon tomato purée	1 teaspoon tomato purée
150 ml dry white wine	$\frac{1}{4}$ pint dry white wine
4 tablespoons water	4 tablespoons water
1 bay leaf	1 bay leaf
salt and pepper	salt and pepper
pinch of sugar	pinch of sugar
1 teaspoon lemon juice	1 teaspoon lemon juice
2 tablespoons apricot jam, sieved	2 tablespoons apricot jam, sieved
300 ml mayonnaise	$\frac{1}{2}$ pint mayonnaise
6 tablespoons double cream	6 tablespoons double cream

If possible, do not carve the chicken until it is completely cold, as it will then be easier to slice and also more moist. Carve into neat slices and put into a bowl. Heat the oil and cook the onion until just soft but not coloured. Stir in the curry powder, tomato purée, wine, water, bay leaf, salt, pepper, sugar, lemon juice and jam. Bring to the boil and then simmer for 10 minutes. Press through a sieve and cool. Stir into the mayonnaise. Whip the cream to soft peaks and fold into the sauce. Put two-thirds of the sauce into the bowl with the chicken and gently coat the chicken with sauce. Arrange the chicken on a serving dish and pour over the remaining sauce.

Serve with a salad of cold boiled rice mixed with cold peas, chopped cucumber, a little chopped pineapple or apricot, a few sultanas, a few chopped nuts and a sprinkling of chopped fresh herbs mixed with an oil and vinegar dressing. Serves 6

Sweet Things

Little Almond Biscuits

METRIC	IMPERIAL
200 g plain flour	7 oz plain flour
25 g ground rice	1 oz ground rice
50 g blanched almonds, chopped	2 oz blanched almonds, chopped
25 g mixed candied peel, chopped	1 oz mixed candied peel, chopped
75 g castor sugar	3 oz castor sugar
125 g butter	5 oz butter
3 drops of almond essence	3 drops of almond essence

Sift together the flour and ground rice. Stir in the almonds, peel and sugar and mix well. Add the butter in small pieces and the almond essence. Work together with the tips of the fingers to make a smooth dough. Press into a greased 18 × 28-cm/7 × 11-inch Swiss roll tin and prick all over with a fork. Bake in a moderate oven (180°C, 350°F, Gas Mark 4) for 30 minutes until golden. Mark into fingers while warm. Leave in the tin until cold, then cut into fingers and lift from the tin.

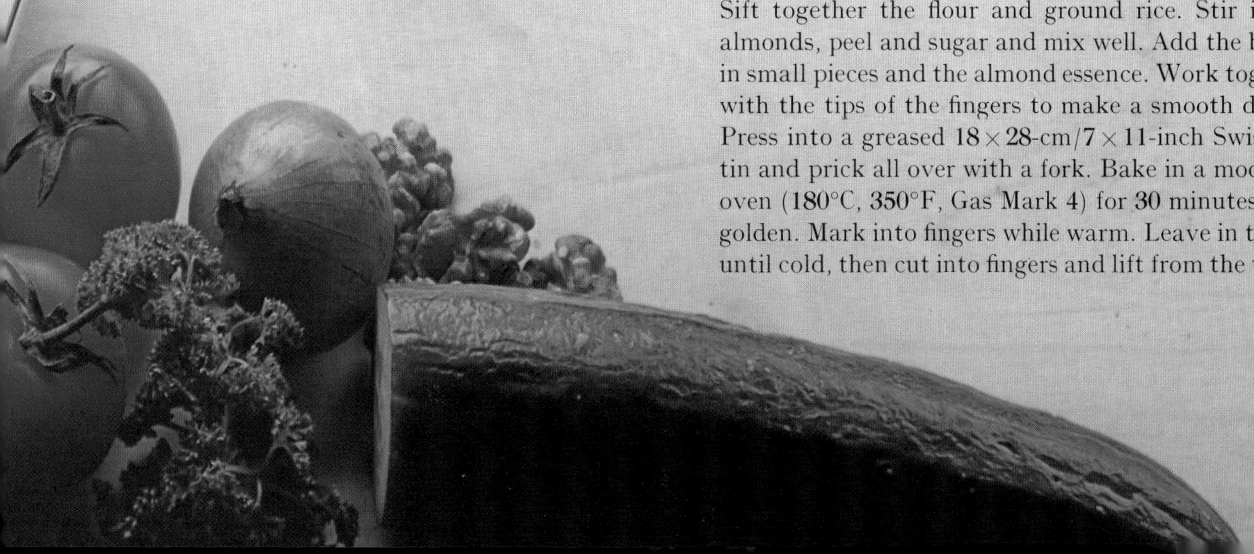

Baked Cheesecake

Serve this light creamy cheesecake with fresh, canned or frozen fruit as a change from the uncooked type of cheesecake.

METRIC	IMPERIAL
50 g digestive biscuits, crumbed	2 oz digestive biscuits, crumbed
450 g cottage cheese	1 lb cottage cheese
1 teaspoon lemon juice	1 teaspoon lemon juice
grated rind of 1 orange	grated rind of 1 orange
15 g cornflour	½ oz cornflour
2 tablespoons double cream	2 tablespoons double cream
2 eggs, separated	2 eggs, separated
100 g castor sugar	4 oz castor sugar

Butter a 20-cm/8-inch round cake tin with a removable base and line the base with greaseproof paper. Butter the paper and sprinkle with the crumbs. Sieve the cottage cheese and stir in the lemon juice, orange rind and cornflour. Whip the cream and stir into the mixture. Beat the egg yolks until thick and stir into the cheese mixture.

Whisk the egg whites to stiff peaks and then beat in half the sugar until the mixture is shiny. Fold in the remaining sugar. Fold this mixture into the cheese. Put into the prepared tin. Bake in a moderate oven (180°C, 350°F, Gas Mark 4) for 1 hour. Turn off the oven and leave the cheesecake to cool in the oven. Remove from the tin and place on a serving plate. Serves 6–8

Gooseberry Sorbet

METRIC	IMPERIAL
900 g green gooseberries	2 lb green gooseberries
175 g sugar	6 oz sugar
900 ml water	1½ pints water
juice of 1 lemon	juice of 1 lemon
few drops of green food colouring	few drops of green food colouring
3 tablespoons light rum	3 tablespoons light rum

Top and tail the gooseberries and put into a pan with the sugar and water. Simmer until the berries are very soft. Put through a sieve and stir in the lemon juice and a little colouring. Cool the purée and then put into an ice tray. Freeze in the ice-making compartment of the refrigerator at the lowest setting for 1 hour. Beat the ice until soft and stir in the rum. Return to the ice tray and continue to freeze for 2 hours. This ice will not become solid. Scoop into glasses and serve with sweet biscuits. Serves 4–6

Gooseberry Sorbet

Baked Cheesecake

Blackcurrant Leaf Ice

Young blackcurrant leaves are very fragrant, and this is a delicately refreshing ice.

METRIC	IMPERIAL
600 ml water	1 pint water
175 g sugar	6 oz sugar
3 large handfuls young blackcurrant leaves	3 large handfuls young blackcurrant leaves
3 lemons	3 lemons
few drops of green food colouring	few drops of green food colouring

Put the water and sugar into a pan and heat gently until the sugar has dissolved completely. Boil for 5 minutes. Add the blackcurrant leaves. Peel 2 of the lemons and add the peel to the syrup. Squeeze the juice from all the lemons and add to the syrup. Cover and remove from the heat. Leave until cold. Drain off the syrup, pressing the leaves to extract all the liquid. Colour very lightly. Pour into an ice-making tray and freeze in the ice-making compartment of the refrigerator at the lowest setting for 1 hour. Stir well and continue freezing for 2 hours. Serve scooped into glasses accompanied by a sweet biscuit. This is delicious with any fresh or frozen fruit. Serves 4

Blackcurrant Leaf Ice

June

This lovely month is for outdoor living, playing games (or watching them) and enjoying cool and refreshing food. There are plenty of new vegetables and gorgeous soft fruit to eat with sugar and cream or to make into delectable dishes. The evenings are long, and it is time to get out the barbecue for casual parties.

Foods in Season

FISH

Brill · Carp · Crab · Crayfish · Haddock · Herring · Lobster · Mullet · Plaice · Prawns
Salmon · Salmon trout · Shrimps · Sole · Trout · Turbot · Whitebait

POULTRY AND GAME

Chicken · Duck · Guinea fowl

VEGETABLES
(home produced and imported)

Asparagus · Broad beans · Cabbage · Cauliflower · Corn-on-the-cob · Courgettes
French beans · Globe artichokes · Peas · Potatoes · Spinach · Tomatoes

FRUIT
(home produced and imported)

Apricots · Cherries · Gooseberries · Lemons · Loganberries · Oranges · Peaches
· Raspberries · Rhubarb · Strawberries

Freezer Notes

Still more vegetables are available, including globe artichokes, French beans and new potatoes, but this is the month for soft fruit, so it is a good idea to keep plenty of freezer space for it. Freeze sweet cherries and cooking cherries, gooseberries and strawberries, and be sure to keep plenty of cream and ice cream in the freezer to go with the fruit which is being eaten freshly-picked.

Soups and Starters

Fresh Pea Soup

METRIC	IMPERIAL
900 g green peas, shelled	2 lb green peas, shelled
25 g butter	1 oz butter
1 small onion, grated	1 small onion, grated
1 small lettuce, shredded	1 small lettuce, shredded
small bunch of fresh mixed herbs	small bunch of fresh mixed herbs
1·75 litres chicken stock	3 pints chicken stock
salt and pepper	salt and pepper
1 teaspoon chopped mint to garnish	1 teaspoon chopped mint to garnish

Put the peas, butter, onion, lettuce and herbs into a pan with a tight-fitting lid. Cook slowly for 10 minutes. Add the stock, salt and pepper and bring to the boil. Cover and simmer for 1½ hours.

Put through a sieve, or purée in a liquidiser. Reheat and serve each bowl garnished with the chopped mint. Serves 4–6

Stuffed Courgettes in Tomato Sauce

METRIC	IMPERIAL
675 g courgettes	1½ lb courgettes
3 tablespoons oil	3 tablespoons oil
1 large onion, chopped	1 large onion, chopped
1 teaspoon salt	1 teaspoon salt
¼ teaspoon black pepper	¼ teaspoon black pepper
pinch of dried marjoram	pinch of dried marjoram
1 clove garlic, crushed	1 clove garlic, crushed
450 g tomatoes	1 lb tomatoes
50 g fresh white breadcrumbs	2 oz fresh white breadcrumbs
25 g butter, softened	1 oz butter, softened
25 g Cheddar cheese, grated	1 oz Cheddar cheese, grated

Wipe the courgettes but do not peel them. Split in half lengthways. Heat the oil and cook the onion over a low heat for 5 minutes. Add the courgettes and cook for 3 minutes on each side. Lift out the courgettes and arrange in an ovenproof dish. Add the salt, pepper, marjoram and garlic to the onions and cook for 1 minute.

Peel the tomatoes and remove the seeds. Chop the flesh finely. Drain the onions and put them into a bowl. Mix with the breadcrumbs, butter and cheese and put a little of this mixture on top of each half courgette. Add the tomatoes to the oil remaining in the pan and simmer for 5 minutes. Season with salt and pepper and pour over the courgettes. Bake in a moderate oven (180°C, 350°F, Gas Mark 4) for 25 minutes. Serve hot or cold as a separate dish, or as an accompaniment to meat or fish. Serves 4–6

Below: Stuffed Courgettes in Tomato Sauce; right: Stuffed Globe Artichokes

Stuffed Globe Artichokes

These artichokes can be served accompanied by melted butter as below, or hollandaise sauce (see page 75).

METRIC	IMPERIAL
4 globe artichokes	4 globe artichokes
100 g cooked ham, minced	4 oz cooked ham, minced
50 g mushrooms, chopped	2 oz mushrooms, chopped
50 g onion, chopped	2 oz onion, chopped
1 clove garlic, crushed	1 clove garlic, crushed
salt and pepper	salt and pepper
300 ml chicken stock	½ pint chicken stock
50 g butter	2 oz butter

To prepare the artichokes, strip off the large outside leaves, trim off the stalks and trim the bases neatly so that the artichokes will stand on a plate. Snip across the end of each leaf to within 5 cm/2 inches of the base. Scoop out the fluffy inner 'choke' with a sharp knife. Put the artichokes base upwards in a bowl of cold salted water for 1 hour to clear away small insects. Drain the artichokes and cook them base upwards in a pan of boiling salted water with a squeeze of lemon juice for about 25 minutes, until an outside leaf will pull out easily. Drain very thoroughly.

Mix together the ham, mushrooms, onion, garlic and a little seasoning, and stuff the artichokes with this mixture. Put the stock into an ovenproof dish and put in the artichokes close together. Cover and cook in a moderate oven (180°C, 350°F, Gas Mark 4) for 25 minutes. Lift on to hot plates. Melt the butter in the cooking liquid and serve as a sauce. Serves 4

Duck and Orange Terrine

Duck and Orange Terrine

METRIC	IMPERIAL
1 (2-kg) duckling	1 (4½-lb) duckling
liver of the duck	liver of the duck
225 g lean pork	8 oz lean pork
1 clove garlic, crushed	1 clove garlic, crushed
pinch of ground mace	pinch of ground mace
pinch of grated nutmeg	pinch of grated nutmeg
salt and pepper	salt and pepper
3 tablespoons dry white wine	3 tablespoons dry white wine
1 tablespoon dry sherry	1 tablespoon dry sherry
2 oranges	2 oranges
150 ml aspic jelly	¼ pint aspic jelly

Prick the duckling all over with a fork and put on a rack in a roasting tin. Roast in a moderate oven (180°C, 350°F, Gas Mark 4) for 1 hour. Strip off all the duck flesh. Mince the duck, liver and pork twice. Mix with the garlic, mace, nutmeg, salt, pepper, wine and sherry. Press this into a lightly greased earthenware dish and cover with a lid or foil.

Put the dish into a roasting tin containing 2·5 cm/1 inch water. Cook in a cool oven (150°C, 300°F, Gas Mark 2) for 1½ hours, until the mixture shrinks from the side of the tin. Cool for 24 hours under weights. Peel the oranges and cut crossways into thin slices. Arrange on top of the pâté. Make up the aspic and leave until cool and syrupy. Pour carefully over the surface. Chill before serving. Serve in slices with salad or toast. Serves 6–8

Iced Camembert

This makes a delicious first course for a summer meal, providing a contrast between the iced cheese and the hot biscuits.

METRIC	IMPERIAL
1 ripe Camembert cheese	1 ripe Camembert cheese
150 ml dry white wine	$\frac{1}{4}$ pint dry white wine
50 g unsalted butter	2 oz unsalted butter
pinch of paprika	pinch of paprika
water biscuits	water biscuits

Scrape the skin carefully from the cheese and put the cheese into a bowl. Mash lightly with a fork and add the wine. Leave to stand for 4 hours. Drain off the wine. Soften the butter slightly and beat into the cheese until the mixture is smooth and creamy. Put into individual ramekins and chill for 4 hours in the coldest part of the refrigerator. Just before serving, heat the biscuits in the oven or under the grill until piping hot. Sprinkle the cheese with a little paprika and serve with the hot biscuits. Serves 4–6

Iced Camembert

Main Dishes

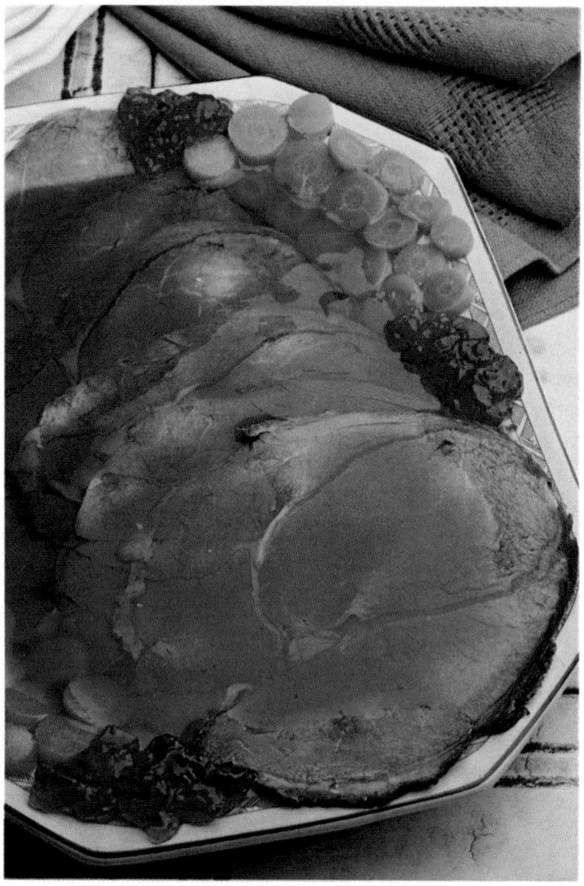

Jellied Beef

Jellied Beef

METRIC	IMPERIAL
2 kg brisket of beef, rolled	4 lb brisket of beef, rolled
600 ml red wine	1 pint red wine
50 g butter	2 oz butter
2 tablespoons oil	2 tablespoons oil
225 g lean bacon, chopped	8 oz lean bacon, chopped
salt and pepper	salt and pepper
300 ml beef stock	½ pint beef stock
pinch of grated nutmeg	pinch of grated nutmeg
1 sprig parsley	1 sprig parsley
1 sprig thyme	1 sprig thyme
1 bay leaf	1 bay leaf
4 medium onions, sliced	4 medium onions, sliced
1 calf's foot, split	1 calf's foot, split
4 carrots, sliced	4 medium carrots, sliced
1 tablespoon chopped parsley	1 tablespoon chopped parsley

The meat should not be too fatty, and must be firmly tied.

Put the meat into a bowl, pour on the wine and leave to stand for 2 hours. Drain the meat well. Heat the butter and oil and brown the meat, turning to seal all sides. Lift the meat into a casserole. Fry the bacon in the remaining fat until just cooked. Drain the bacon and add to the beef. Add all the other ingredients except the carrots and parsley. Cover and cook in a moderate oven (160°C, 325°F, Gas Mark 3) for 2 hours.

Add the carrots, cover and continue cooking for 1 hour. Cool for 30 minutes and carve the beef into neat slices. Arrange the beef on a serving dish. Strain the cooking liquid and arrange the carrots on the meat. Cool the liquid and skim off the fat. Reheat, cool slightly and pour over the beef and carrots. Chill well. Sprinkle with the freshly chopped parsley just before serving. Serves 8–10

Tongue in Vegetable Aspic

The secret of preparing an attractive jellied dish is to arrange each layer and let it set before adding the next one, so that the finished dish consists of neat, colourful stripes which look attractive when the dish is sliced.

METRIC	IMPERIAL
475 ml aspic jelly	¾ pint aspic jelly
1 egg, hard-boiled	1 egg, hard-boiled
350 g tongue, sliced	12 oz tongue, sliced
350 g summer vegetables, cooked	12 oz summer vegetables, cooked

The vegetables for this dish should be small and colourful, such as a mixture of green peas, chopped French beans, sliced baby carrots and sweet corn kernels. Make the aspic in an 18-cm/7-inch soufflé dish if possible, as it will then turn out in a neat shape.

Make up the aspic jelly and cool until it is just syrupy, rather like uncooked egg white. Pour a little into the dish to give a layer about 1 cm/½ inch deep. Chill in the ice-making compartment of the refrigerator for a few minutes until set firmly. Slice the egg in thin rounds and arrange on this jellied layer. Pour in just enough aspic to cover the eggs and set quickly again. Cut the tongue into bite-sized pieces and put half of them into the dish, covering with aspic. Set quickly, then top with half the vegetables and more aspic. Add more tongue and aspic, then finally the remaining vegetables and aspic. Chill until firm, and turn out on to a serving dish. Serve in wedges. Serves 4–6

Tongue in Vegetable Aspic

Summer Veal Casserole

METRIC	IMPERIAL
450 g pie veal, cubed	1 lb pie veal, cubed
3 tablespoons olive oil	3 tablespoons olive oil
2 medium onions, chopped	2 medium onions, chopped
25 g plain flour	1 oz plain flour
150 ml white wine	$\frac{1}{4}$ pint white wine
300 ml stock	$\frac{1}{2}$ pint stock
100 g button mushrooms	4 oz button mushrooms
2 tablespoons tomato purée	2 tablespoons tomato purée
1 clove garlic, crushed	1 clove garlic, crushed
225 g green peas, shelled	8 oz green peas, shelled
salt and pepper	salt and pepper
12 stuffed green olives	12 stuffed green olives

Fry the veal in the oil until golden. Add the onions and fry for 5 minutes, stirring well. Sprinkle in the flour and cook for 3 minutes. Stir in the wine and stock and bring to the boil. Add the whole mushrooms, tomato purée and garlic.

Cover and cook in a moderate oven (160°C, 325°F, Gas Mark 3) for 45 minutes. Add the peas, salt and pepper. Cover and continue cooking for 20 minutes. Stir in the olives, and serve very hot with new potatoes or rice. Serves 4

Summer Veal Casserole

Bacon and Kidney Kebabs

Food threaded on skewers is ideal for a barbecue, but the kebabs can easily be cooked under a hot grill for a more formal meal.

METRIC	IMPERIAL
8 lamb's kidneys	8 lamb's kidneys
8 rashers streaky bacon	8 rashers streaky bacon
8 small tomatoes	8 small tomatoes
16 button mushrooms	16 button mushrooms
4 bay leaves	4 bay leaves
salt and pepper	salt and pepper
pinch of thyme	pinch of thyme
olive oil	olive oil
Sauce	*Sauce*
2 tablespoons tomato ketchup	2 tablespoons tomato ketchup
1 tablespoon vinegar	1 tablespoon vinegar
2 teaspoons Worcestershire sauce	2 teaspoons Worcestershire sauce
½ teaspoon made mustard	½ teaspoon made mustard
1 tablespoon lemon juice	1 tablespoon lemon juice
1 tablespoon light soft brown sugar	1 tablespoon light soft brown sugar

Remove the skins and cores from the kidneys and split them in half. Cut the bacon in squares. Thread the kidney halves, bacon squares, whole tomatoes and mushrooms on four long, smooth skewers, putting the bay leaves halfway along. Season well with salt, pepper and thyme. Brush lightly with olive oil. Grill for 5 minutes under a hot grill, turning the skewers once.

Mix the sauce ingredients together and brush all over the skewered ingredients. Continue grilling for 5 minutes, turning once. Heat the remaining sauce very gently and pour over the kebabs just before serving. Serve with salad and rice, or with soft baps for a barbecue. Serves 4

Chicken and Ham Pie

METRIC	IMPERIAL
350 g shortcrust pastry	12 oz shortcrust pastry
450 g uncooked chicken	1 lb uncooked chicken
100 g uncooked ham	4 oz uncooked ham
2 teaspoons lemon juice	2 teaspoons lemon juice
pinch of dried thyme	pinch of dried thyme
150 ml water	¼ pint water
salt and pepper	salt and pepper
beaten egg to glaze	beaten egg to glaze

Roll out the pastry, and use half to line a 23-cm/9-inch pie plate. Strip the chicken flesh from a whole bird or from chicken joints to make the required amount, and cut into neat cubes. Cut the ham into strips. Mix the two meats together with the lemon juice, thyme, water and seasoning. Put into the pastry case and cover with the remaining pastry. Use the pastry trimmings to make leaves and arrange these on top of the pie. Make a small hole in the centre of the lid. Brush with beaten egg to glaze.

Bake in a moderately hot oven (190°C, 375°F, Gas Mark 5) for 30 minutes, and reduce the heat to moderate (180°C, 350°F, Gas Mark 4) for 30 minutes. Serve hot with vegetables, or cold with salad. Serves 6

Far right: Seafood Vols-au-Vent; top: Chicken and Ham Pie; bottom: Bacon and Kidney Kebabs

Seafood Vols-au-Vent

METRIC	IMPERIAL
225 g frozen puff pastry	8 oz frozen puff pastry
15 g butter	½ oz butter
15 g plain flour	½ oz plain flour
150 ml milk	¼ pint milk
100 g smoked haddock, cooked and flaked	4 oz smoked haddock, cooked and flaked
100 g peeled prawns	4 oz peeled prawns
50 g Cheddar cheese, grated	2 oz Cheddar cheese, grated
1 tablespoon chopped parsley	1 tablespoon chopped parsley
salt and pepper	salt and pepper

Roll out the pastry and cut six 7·5-cm/3-inch rounds. Mark a 3·75-cm/1½-inch circle in the centre of each. Put on a baking tray rinsed in cold water and bake in a hot oven (220°C, 425°F, Gas Mark 7) for 15 minutes until well-risen and golden brown.

Prepare the filling while the pastry is cooking. Melt the butter, stir in the flour and cook for 1 minute. Stir in the milk gradually and cook over a low heat, stirring well, until thick and creamy. Stir in the haddock, prawns, cheese, parsley and seasoning and heat through. Use a pointed knife to remove the lids from the pastry cases. Divide the filling between the cases and replace the lids. Heat in a moderate oven (180°C, 350°F, Gas Mark 4) for 10 minutes and serve hot. Serves 6

Strawberry Layer; Strawberry Flan

Sweet Things

Strawberry Layer

METRIC	IMPERIAL
150 ml double cream	¼ pint double cream
1 (142-ml) carton natural yogurt	1 (5-fl oz) carton natural yogurt
50 g castor sugar	2 oz castor sugar
100 g shortbread biscuits	4 oz shortbread biscuits
75 g strawberry jam	3 oz strawberry jam
1 teaspoon lemon juice	1 teaspoon lemon juice
2 teaspoons orange liqueur	2 teaspoons orange liqueur
225 g strawberries	8 oz strawberries

Have ready four tall glasses or six large wine glasses. Whip the cream to soft peaks and fold in the yogurt and sugar. Crush the biscuits with a rolling pin into coarse crumbs. Mix the jam, lemon juice and liqueur.

Wipe the strawberries clean and reserve 4 or 6 for decoration. Cut the rest into quarters, cutting downwards. Put half the jam mixture into the glasses. Top with half the cream mixture, then half the crumbs and half the strawberries. Add half the remaining cream mixture, then the remaining jam, crumbs and strawberries. Finish with the remaining cream and top each glass with a whole strawberry. Serve thoroughly chilled. Serves 4–6

Strawberry Flan

The pastry for fresh fruit flans should be slightly sweet and rather crumbly, so it may be a little difficult to roll out, and should be handled with care. Raspberries or grapes may be used instead of strawberries, but they all go well with whipped cream flavoured with kirsch.

METRIC	IMPERIAL
175 g plain flour	6 oz plain flour
¼ teaspoon salt	¼ teaspoon salt
75 g butter	3 oz butter
25 g castor sugar	1 oz castor sugar
1 egg yolk	1 egg yolk
1 tablespoon cold water	1 tablespoon cold water
450 g strawberries	1 lb strawberries
2 tablespoons redcurrant jelly	2 tablespoons redcurrant jelly

Sift together the flour and salt. Rub in the butter until the mixture is like fine breadcrumbs. Stir in the sugar. Mix the egg yolk and water together and add to the flour to make a firm dough. Knead lightly on a floured board. Roll out the pastry to fit a 20-cm/8-inch flan ring. Prick the bottom of the pastry and press a piece of kitchen foil over the surface. Bake in a moderately hot oven (200°C, 400°F, Gas Mark 6) for 25 minutes until light golden. Leave until cold.

Hull the strawberries and wipe them clean. Put into the pastry case, points upward and with the largest berries in the centre. Melt the jelly and spoon over the fruit. Eat freshly baked. Serves 6

Raspberry Mille Feuilles

METRIC	IMPERIAL
350 g frozen puff pastry	12 oz frozen puff pastry
3 tablespoons raspberry jam	3 tablespoons raspberry jam
2 teaspoons kirsch	2 teaspoons kirsch
150 ml double cream	¼ pint double cream
2 teaspoons castor sugar	2 teaspoons castor sugar
350 g raspberries	12 oz raspberries
75 g icing sugar	3 oz icing sugar

Roll out the pastry to a 20 × 25-cm/8 × 10-inch rectangle. Cut into three strips lengthwise and put on a baking tray rinsed in cold water. Bake in a hot oven (220°C, 425°F, Gas Mark 7) for 20 minutes until the pastry is well risen and crisp. Lift on to a wire rack to cool. Using a very sharp knife, trim the pastry into three equal rectangles. Crush the trimmings lightly with a rolling pin.

Mix the jam and kirsch and spread on top of two of the pastry pieces. Whip the cream to soft peaks and stir in the castor sugar. Put one piece of pastry on a serving plate. Top the jam with half the cream and half the raspberries. Put on the second piece of pastry and top the jam with the remaining cream and fruit. Put the plain piece of pastry on top. Sift the icing sugar and add just enough water to make a smooth thick icing. Spread over the surface of the pastry. Sprinkle the pastry crumbs in a 2·5-cm/1-inch border on top of the icing. Serve freshly baked. Serves 4–6

Raspberry Mille Feuilles

Banana Bread

METRIC	IMPERIAL
225 g plain flour	8 oz plain flour
pinch of salt	pinch of salt
1 teaspoon bicarbonate of soda	1 teaspoon bicarbonate of soda
125 g butter	5 oz butter
100 g castor sugar	4 oz castor sugar
3 eggs	3 eggs
2 ripe bananas	2 ripe bananas
25 g walnuts, chopped	1 oz walnuts, chopped
2 tablespoons milk	2 tablespoons milk
1 tablespoon lemon juice	1 tablespoon lemon juice

Sift the flour, salt and bicarbonate of soda together. Cream the butter and sugar until light and fluffy. Beat in the eggs one at a time, adding a little flour with each. Mash the bananas with a fork. Stir the bananas and nuts into the mixture and then fold in the remaining flour alternately with the milk and lemon juice.

Turn into a greased 18-cm/7-inch square tin, base-lined with greaseproof paper. Bake in a moderate oven (180°C, 350°F, Gas Mark 4) for 50 minutes until firm and well risen. Cool on a wire rack. Serve in thin slices spread with butter.

Above: Luscious Lemon Cake; above right: Petticoat Tails

Luscious Lemon Cake

METRIC	IMPERIAL
40 g butter	1½ oz butter
175 g castor sugar	6 oz castor sugar
3 egg yolks	3 egg yolks
¼ teaspoon lemon essence	¼ teaspoon lemon essence
175 g self-raising flour	6 oz self-raising flour
6 tablespoons milk	6 tablespoons milk
pinch of salt	pinch of salt
Icing	*Icing*
3 tablespoons soft butter	3 tablespoons soft butter
1 tablespoon grated orange rind	1 tablespoon grated orange rind
350 g icing sugar	12 oz icing sugar
2 tablespoons lemon juice	2 tablespoons lemon juice
1 tablespoon water	1 tablespoon water
pinch of salt	pinch of salt

Cream the butter until light and gradually work in the sugar, egg yolks and lemon essence. Sift the flour and add alternately with the milk. Add the salt and beat well. Put into two 20-cm/8-inch sandwich tins, base-lined with greaseproof paper. Bake in a moderate oven (180°C, 350°F, Gas Mark 4) for 25 minutes. Turn out and cool on a wire rack.

To make the icing, cream the butter and orange rind. Sift in a third of the icing sugar and cream thoroughly. Mix the lemon juice and water, and add to the mixture alternately with the remaining sifted icing sugar. Add the salt and beat well until fluffy. Sandwich the cakes with the icing. Spoon or pipe the rest on top of the cake.

Banana Bread

Petticoat Tails

These little crisp shortbread biscuits were great favourites of Mary, Queen of Scots. They look like the edges of petticoats, and are very good with tea or coffee, or with ices or fruit dishes.

METRIC	IMPERIAL
300 g plain flour	11 oz plain flour
50 g rice flour	2 oz rice flour
150 g butter	5 oz butter
4 tablespoons milk	4 tablespoons milk
50 g castor sugar	2 oz castor sugar
castor sugar to sprinkle	castor sugar to sprinkle

Sift the flour and rice flour together in a bowl, and make a well in the middle. Heat the butter and milk together until the butter has just melted. Pour into the flour and add the sugar. Mix with the fingers and knead very lightly to a dough. Put on to a lightly floured board, and roll into a circle about 5 mm/¼ inch thick.

Put an inverted dinner plate on top and cut round the edge with a sharp knife. Remove the dinner plate. Invert a wineglass in the centre of the circle of dough, and cut round this to make a small circle. Keep the centre unmarked, but mark the remaining outer circle into eight segments, making a deep incision but not cutting right through the dough. Put a piece of greased greaseproof paper on a baking tray and lift the two circles of dough on to it. Bake in a moderate oven (180°C, 350°F, Gas Mark 4) for 20 minutes until pale golden. Cool on a wire rack. Assemble the biscuits on a large flat serving plate with the circle in the centre and the triangular pieces around it. Dust lightly with castor sugar.

Summer Drinks

Iced Coffee

METRIC	IMPERIAL
40 g ground coffee	1½ oz ground coffee
600 ml boiling water	1 pint boiling water
6 cubes sugar	6 cubes sugar
1·15 litres milk, chilled	2 pints milk, chilled
whipped cream or ice cream (optional)	whipped cream or ice cream (optional)

Pour the water on to the coffee, stir well and leave to stand for 4 minutes. Strain into a non-metal container, cover tightly and chill in the refrigerator. Do not leave to stand longer than 3 hours, or the coffee will lose its flavour. Mix the coffee, sugar and milk together and either mix in a liquidiser, or whisk with an egg whisk to make the mixture light and foamy. Pour into tall glasses and serve with straws. If liked, top with a swirl of whipped cream or a scoop of vanilla or coffee ice cream. Serves 6

Old-Fashioned Lemonade

Home-made lemonade is far more refreshing than the bought variety. It should be stored in the refrigerator, and will keep for two weeks. Dilute to taste with iced water on a hot day (the drink is just as good in winter when mixed with boiling water).

METRIC	IMPERIAL
900 g granulated sugar	2 lb granulated sugar
4 large lemons	4 large lemons
2 teaspoons tartaric acid	2 teaspoons tartaric acid
1·15 litres water	2 pints water

Put the sugar into a large bowl. Cut the lemons in half and squeeze all the juice on to the sugar. Stir well and add the tartaric acid. Boil the water and pour on to the sugar. Stir well until the sugar has dissolved. Leave until cold. Pour into bottles and store in the refrigerator.

Old-Fashioned Lemonade

Iced Coffee

Cider Fruit Cup

This is a refreshing and inexpensive drink for a party. On the day before the party, make a large block of ice in a freezer container, as this will cool the drink without diluting it as quickly as small ice cubes.

METRIC	IMPERIAL
2·25 litres dry cider	4 pints dry cider
½ bottle orange squash	½ bottle orange squash
½ bottle lemon squash	½ bottle lemon squash
600 ml pineapple juice	1 pint pineapple juice
150 ml sweet sherry	¼ pint sweet sherry
dash of Angostura bitters	dash of Angostura bitters
225 g strawberries, halved	8 oz strawberries, halved
few fresh mint leaves	few fresh mint leaves

Mix together the cider, orange squash, lemon squash, and pineapple juice. Leave to stand in a cold place for 2 hours. Put the sherry and bitters into a bowl and add the strawberries. Leave to stand in a cold place for 2 hours.

Just before serving, mix the strawberries and their liquid with the cider mixture. Put a large block of ice into a serving bowl. Pour over the cider cup and garnish with mint leaves. Serves 15

Cider Fruit Cup

July

In hot weather, appetites are small, but it is easy to make delicious salads and tempting vegetable dishes. All kinds of soft fruit are available for sweet dishes and for jams and jellies which will brighten meals during the winter.

Foods in Season

FISH

Brill · Carp · Crab · Crayfish · Haddock · Halibut · Herring · Lobster · Mullet · Plaice
Prawns · Salmon · Salmon trout · Shrimps · Sole · Trout · Turbot · Whitebait

POULTRY AND GAME

Chicken · Duck

VEGETABLES
(home produced and imported)

Aubergines · Broad beans · Cabbage · Carrots · Cauliflower · Corn-on-the-cob · Courgettes
French beans · Globe artichokes · Peas · Peppers · Potatoes · Spinach · Tomatoes

FRUIT
(home produced and imported)

Apricots · Blackcurrants · Cherries · Figs · Gooseberries · Lemons · Loganberries · Melons
Nectarines · Oranges · Peaches · Plums · Raspberries · Redcurrants · Rhubarb
Strawberries

Freezer Notes

This is the month when there is an enormous amount of fruit and vegetables to be frozen. Aubergines, peppers and courgettes are in good supply and top condition, as well as all the garden vegetables. Blackcurrants, redcurrants and raspberries can be easily frozen in dry sugar if time is short. Imported peaches, melons and apricots are all available and are best preserved in syrup. This is also a good month for fish and shellfish, and those with gardens may like to freeze herbs.

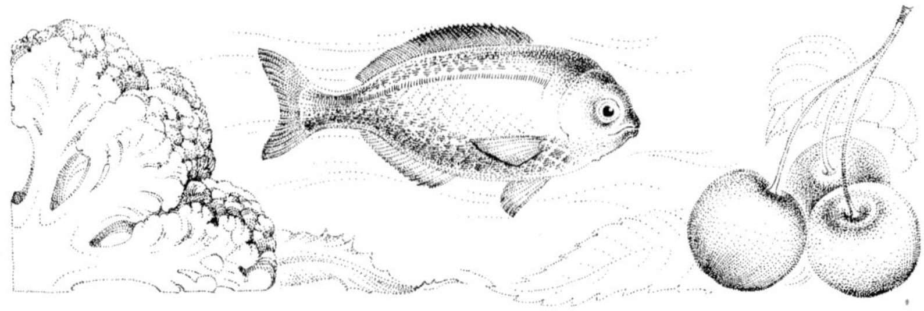

Above: Kippered Mackerel Vinaigrette; right: Sardine Pâté

Starters

Kippered Mackerel Vinaigrette

Kippered mackerel fillets may be bought fresh or frozen. They are plump with a rich flavour, and this dish is excellent for a first course, or may be served with salad and plenty of wholemeal bread

METRIC	IMPERIAL
8 fillets kippered mackerel	8 fillets kippered mackerel
1 medium onion	1 medium onion
6 tablespoons oil	6 tablespoons oil
3 tablespoons vinegar	3 tablespoons vinegar
salt and pepper	salt and pepper
1 tablespoon chopped parsley	1 tablespoon chopped parsley

Skin the fillets. Leave whole or cut in 2·5-cm/1-inch wide slices. Arrange in a shallow serving dish. Peel the onion and cut it in very thin slices. Break the slices into rings and arrange these on top of the fish. Mix together the oil, vinegar, salt and pepper and pour over the fish. Sprinkle with chopped parsley and chill for 12 hours. Serves 4

Sardine Pâté

METRIC	IMPERIAL
1 (227-g) can sardines in oil	1 (8-oz) can sardines in oil
juice of $\frac{1}{2}$ lemon	juice of $\frac{1}{2}$ lemon
salt and pepper	salt and pepper
pinch of grated nutmeg	pinch of grated nutmeg
50 g butter, melted	2 oz butter, melted
1 bay leaf to garnish	1 bay leaf to garnish

Put the sardines, including the skin, bones and oil, into a bowl or liquidiser. Pound or blend with the lemon juice, salt, pepper and nutmeg until smooth. Press into a dish, cover with the melted butter, and garnish with the bay leaf. Chill before serving with toast or crispbread. Serves 4

Potted Trout

If trout are not available, this recipe may be made with herring or mackerel.

METRIC	IMPERIAL
6 (225-g) trout	6 (8-oz) trout
50 g salt	2 oz salt
1 teaspoon grated nutmeg	1 teaspoon grated nutmeg
1 teaspoon ground cloves	1 teaspoon ground cloves
pinch of ground ginger	pinch of ground ginger
2 bay leaves	2 bay leaves
2 strips lemon peel	2 strips lemon peel
100 g butter	4 oz butter
100 g clarified butter	4 oz clarified butter

Wipe the fish and remove the heads, tails and fins. Remove the backbones and roes. Mix the salt, nutmeg, cloves and ginger and rub into the fish on both sides. Arrange the fish in a single layer in an earthenware dish, and put the bay leaves and lemon peel on top. Cut the butter into flakes and spread over the fish. Cover with a piece of kitchen foil. Bake in a moderate oven (180°C, 350°F, Gas Mark 4) for 40 minutes.

Leave to cool for 20 minutes. Remove the fish skins. Flake the flesh and press into six individual pots, mixing well with a little of the cooking liquid so that the flesh is moist. Chill for 1 hour. Melt the clarified butter and pour on to the surface of each pot. Chill for 2 hours. Serve with salad or toast. Serves 6

Potted Trout

Ratatouille

This is a delicious mixture of summer vegetables which may be eaten hot or cold. It may be used as a first course, or as an accompaniment to meat or fish, with some crusty bread. The mixture freezes very well and may be reheated, or thawed and served cold.

METRIC	IMPERIAL
2 large onions	2 large onions
2 green or red peppers	2 green or red peppers
2 large aubergines	2 large aubergines
3 courgettes	3 courgettes
150 ml olive oil	¼ pint olive oil
4 large tomatoes	4 large tomatoes
2 cloves garlic, crushed	2 cloves garlic, crushed
salt and pepper	salt and pepper

Slice the onions thinly. Remove the cores and seeds from the peppers, and cut the flesh into thin strips. Do not peel the aubergines or courgettes, but slice them thinly. Arrange the slices in a colander in layers with plenty of salt. Leave to stand for 1 hour, then drain very thoroughly and dry well. Heat the oil in a heavy pan and cook the onions gently for 10 minutes. Add the prepared vegetables and continue simmering for 30 minutes with a lid on the pan. Chop the tomatoes and add to the vegetables with the garlic, salt and pepper. Cover and simmer for 45 minutes until the oil has been absorbed. Serve either hot or cold. Serves 4–6

Main Dishes

Bacon in a Pastry Case with Redcurrant Sauce

METRIC	IMPERIAL
25 g butter	1 oz butter
1 medium onion, chopped	1 medium onion, chopped
100 g mushrooms, sliced	4 oz mushrooms, sliced
450 g shortcrust pastry	1 lb shortcrust pastry
salt and pepper	salt and pepper
1 (675-g) vacuum pack bacon joint	1 (1½-lb) vacuum pack bacon joint
beaten egg to glaze	beaten egg to glaze
Sauce	*Sauce*
225 g redcurrants	8 oz redcurrants
75 g sugar	3 oz sugar
150 ml water	¼ pint water

Ratatouille

Melt the butter and cook the onion for 5 minutes until soft and golden. Add the mushrooms and cook for 5 minutes. Leave to cool.

1 · Roll out the pastry to a large circle and spread with the onion and mushroom mixture. Season lightly with salt and pepper. Put the bacon joint in the centre of the pastry.

2 · Bring up the pastry to cover the joint, sealing the edges.

3 · Put on to a baking tray so that the join is underneath. Beat the egg with a pinch of salt and brush the pastry with it. If there are any pastry trimmings, arrange in a leaf pattern on top of the pastry case and brush with egg.

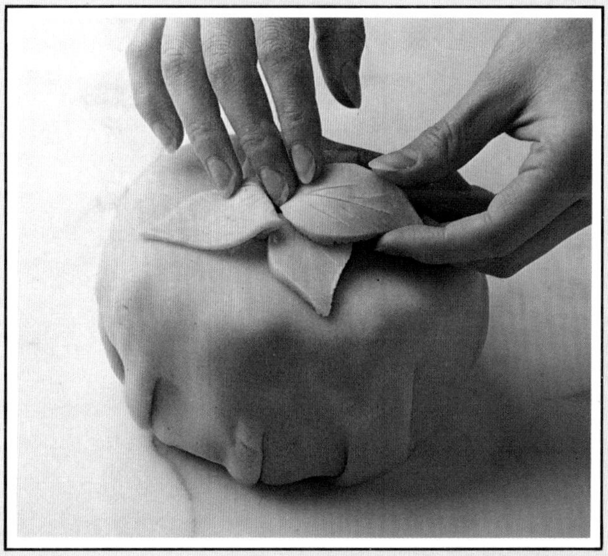

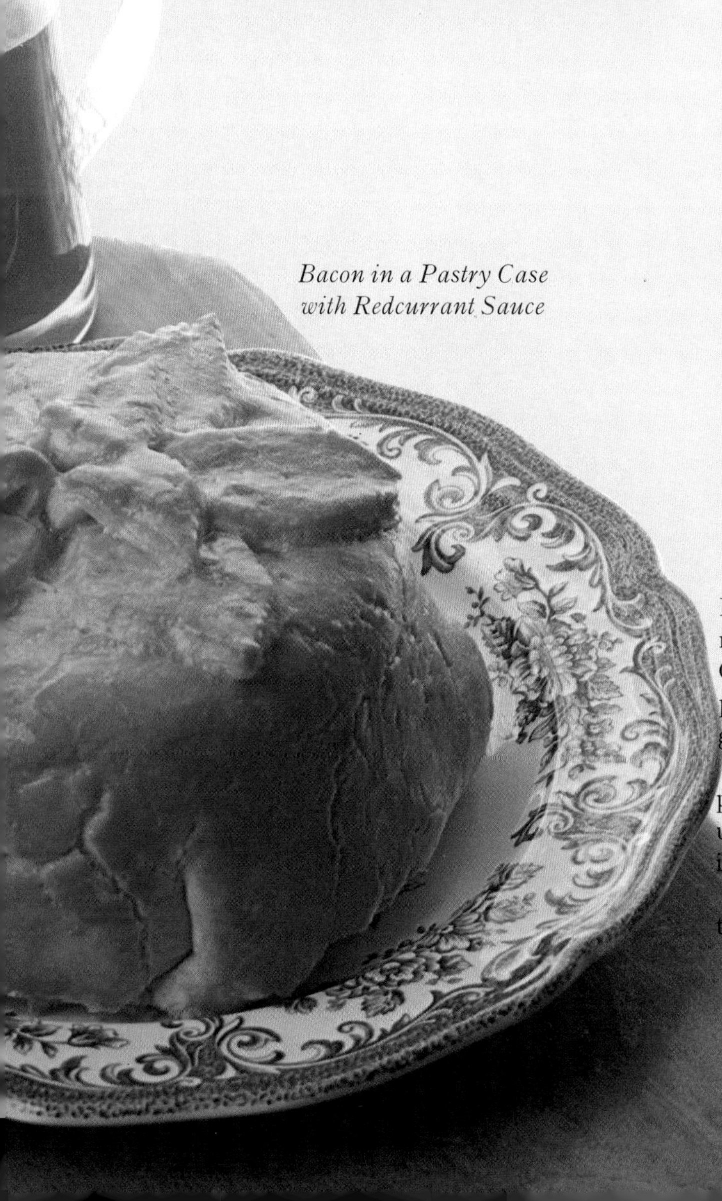

Bacon in a Pastry Case with Redcurrant Sauce

Bake in a hot oven (220°C, 425°F, Gas Mark 7) for 15 minutes. Reduce to a moderate oven (160°C, 325°F, Gas Mark 3) and continue cooking for 1½ hours. If the pastry browns too quickly, cover with a piece of greaseproof paper.

Strip the redcurrants from their stalks. Put into a pan with the sugar and water and stir over a low heat until the sugar dissolves. Simmer for 15 minutes. Pour into a sauceboat and leave until cold.

Lift the bacon on to a serving plate and serve with the redcurrant sauce. Serves 4–6

Summer Beef Galantine

Summer Beef Galantine

METRIC	IMPERIAL
350 g fresh minced beef	12 oz fresh minced beef
100 g streaky bacon, chopped	4 oz streaky bacon, chopped
1 medium onion, grated	1 medium onion, grated
50 g fresh white breadcrumbs	2 oz fresh white breadcrumbs
75 g shredded suet	3 oz shredded suet
1 teaspoon dried mixed herbs	1 teaspoon dried mixed herbs
1 tablespoon tomato ketchup	1 tablespoon tomato ketchup
1 egg	1 egg

Put the mince into a bowl with the bacon and onion. Mix well and then stir in all the other ingredients. Mix thoroughly and form into a large sausage shape. Take a piece of clean cotton or linen, dip it in water and then dust one side lightly with flour. Put the sausage on the floured side and cover it completely with the cloth. Tie the ends with string. Steam for 2½ hours. Unwrap and cool completely. For an attractive appearance, roll the galantine in some crisp browned breadcrumbs. Serve in slices with salad, or use in sandwiches. Serves 4–6

Summer Paella

METRIC	IMPERIAL
2 chicken joints	2 chicken joints
1 (225-g) piece garlic sausage	1 (8-oz) piece garlic sausage
225 g lean pork	8 oz lean pork
3 tablespoons oil	3 tablespoons oil
1 medium onion, chopped	1 medium onion, chopped
3 tomatoes, peeled	3 tomatoes, peeled
450 g long-grain rice	1 lb long-grain rice
225 g shelled peas	8 oz shelled peas
1 red pepper, chopped	1 red pepper, chopped
salt and pepper	salt and pepper
pinch of saffron or turmeric	pinch of saffron or turmeric
225 g peeled prawns	8 oz peeled prawns

Skin the chicken joints and cut the flesh into small cubes. Cut the garlic sausage and the pork into cubes. Heat the oil in a deep pan and add the chicken, pork and sausage. Cook for 5 minutes over a low heat. Add the onion and continue cooking for 5 minutes, stirring well. Chop the tomatoes and add to the mixture. Cook for 3 minutes, then put in the rice and cook for 5 minutes. Add the peas, red pepper, salt, pepper and saffron or turmeric. Stir well and add 900 ml/$1\frac{1}{2}$ pints water. Bring to the boil, then simmer for about 20 minutes, until the liquid is all absorbed and the rice is tender. Stir often during the cooking. Adjust the seasoning and stir in the prawns. Put into a serving dish and leave in a moderate oven (160°C, 325°F, Gas Mark 3) for 5 minutes. If liked garnish with unpeeled prawns and serve with a green salad. Serves 4–6

Summer Paella

Salads

Niçoise Salad

This salad looks most attractive if the ingredients are arranged in layers in a bowl, topped with a lattice of olives and anchovies. The salad should be tossed just before serving.

METRIC	IMPERIAL
1 (198-g) can tuna, drained	1 (7-oz) can tuna, drained
50 g peeled prawns	2 oz peeled prawns
225 g French beans, cooked and cut in chunks	8 oz French beans, cooked and cut in chunks
½ cucumber	½ cucumber
450 g tomatoes, peeled and quartered	1 lb tomatoes, peeled and quartered
3 eggs, hard-boiled	3 eggs, hard-boiled
1 teaspoon chopped fresh herbs	1 teaspoon chopped fresh herbs
50 g black olives	2 oz black olives
8 canned anchovy fillets	8 canned anchovy fillets
150 ml French dressing	¼ pint French dressing

Break the tuna into small chunks and put into a deep salad bowl. Add the prawns and French beans. Do not peel the cucumber, but cut it into small cubes. Put into the bowl with the tomatoes. Cut the eggs in quarters lengthwise and put in the bowl. Sprinkle with the herbs. Arrange the olives and anchovy fillets in a lattice pattern on top of the salad and pour on the French dressing. Serves 4

Spanish New Potato Salad

METRIC	IMPERIAL
450 g small new potatoes	1 lb small new potatoes
1 small onion, chopped	1 small onion, chopped
1 red pepper, chopped	1 red pepper, chopped
6 tablespoons olive oil	6 tablespoons olive oil
3 tablespoons vinegar	3 tablespoons vinegar
salt and pepper	salt and pepper
12 stuffed olives to garnish	12 stuffed olives to garnish

Niçoise Salad

Scrape the new potatoes and boil them for about 12 minutes, until just tender. Meanwhile prepare the onion and pepper, chopping them finely. Mix the oil, vinegar, salt and pepper together. Drain the potatoes and put them into a serving bowl. Sprinkle with onion and pepper and pour on the dressing while the potatoes are still warm. Toss well. Finish with sliced olives just before serving. Serves 4

Green Mayonnaise

This mayonnaise looks and tastes delicious with salads, but it is also very good with fish dishes.

METRIC	IMPERIAL
3 egg yolks	3 egg yolks
salt and pepper	salt and pepper
½ teaspoon French mustard	½ teaspoon French mustard
1 tablespoon lemon juice or white wine vinegar	1 tablespoon lemon juice or white wine vinegar
300 ml salad oil	½ pint salad oil
4 tablespoons watercress leaves	4 tablespoons watercress leaves
2 tablespoons chopped parsley	2 tablespoons chopped parsley
25 g spinach leaves	1 oz spinach leaves

Put the egg yolks, salt, pepper, mustard and lemon juice or vinegar into a bowl, and stir them together. Add the oil drop by drop, beating constantly until all the oil has been incorporated and the mixture is thick and creamy.

Put the watercress, parsley and spinach into a pan and just cover with water. Boil for 5 minutes until the leaves are very tender. Drain off any surplus liquid and rub the leaves through a sieve. Cool and then fold into the mayonnaise with 1 tablespoon boiling water. Keep cool but do not refrigerate.

Below left: Spanish New Potato Salad;
below: Green Mayonnaise

Sweet Things

Raspberry Summer Pudding

All the summer soft fruits go well together, and the strawberry sauce can also be used with currants or with a fruit sorbet.

METRIC	IMPERIAL
450 g raspberries	1 lb raspberries
150 ml sweet cider	¼ pint sweet cider
175 g castor sugar	6 oz castor sugar
5 large slices white bread, cut medium thick	5 large slices white bread, cut medium thick
Strawberry sauce	*Strawberry sauce*
225 g strawberries	8 oz strawberries
175 g sugar	6 oz sugar
6 tablespoons water	6 tablespoons water
1 teaspoon lemon juice	1 teaspoon lemon juice

Put the raspberries, cider and sugar together in a pan and simmer until the fruit is soft. Remove the crusts from the bread. Use four bread slices to line a lightly greased pudding basin, overlapping the edges slightly and making sure the bottom of the basin is covered. Cool the fruit until lukewarm and pour it into the basin. Cover with the last piece of bread. Put a saucer on top and a heavy weight. Leave in a cold place for 24 hours.

Put the strawberries, sugar and water into a pan and simmer until the fruit is soft. Put through a sieve, stir in the lemon juice and chill. Turn the pudding out on to a serving dish. Pour over the sauce just before serving. Serves 4–6

Baking

Summer Vegetable Quiche

The cheese pastry used for this quiche goes particularly well with the creamy vegetable filling. Leftovers may be used, or freshly cooked vegetables.

METRIC	IMPERIAL
175 g white or wholemeal flour	6 oz white or wholemeal flour
pinch of salt	pinch of salt
½ teaspoon dry mustard	½ teaspoon dry mustard
pinch of cayenne pepper	pinch of cayenne pepper
75 g margarine	3 oz margarine
75 g Cheddar cheese, finely grated	3 oz Cheddar cheese, finely grated
2 tablespoons iced water	2 tablespoons iced water
350 g cooked summer vegetables, e.g. carrots, peas, beans, cauliflower florets	12 oz cooked summer vegetables, e.g. carrots, peas, beans, cauliflower florets
1 egg	1 egg
300 ml creamy milk	½ pint creamy milk
salt and pepper	salt and pepper
1 tablespoon grated Parmesan cheese	1 tablespoon grated Parmesan cheese

Stir the flour, salt and mustard together with the cayenne. Rub in the margarine until the mixture is like fine breadcrumbs. Stir in the Cheddar cheese and mix with the water to a firm dough. Chill the pastry for 30 minutes. Roll out the pastry and use to line a 20-cm/8-inch flan ring. Bake blind in a moderately hot oven (200°C, 400°F, Gas Mark 6) for 15 minutes. Arrange the cooked vegetables in the base of the flan. Beat together the egg, milk, salt and pepper. Pour over the vegetables and sprinkle with the Parmesan cheese. Bake for 30–35 minutes until golden. Serves 4–6

Cheese and Herb Bread

METRIC	IMPERIAL
225 g self-raising flour	8 oz self-raising flour
½ teaspoon salt	½ teaspoon salt
pinch of pepper	pinch of pepper
25 g butter	1 oz butter
100 g Cheddar cheese, grated	4 oz Cheddar cheese, grated
1 tablespoon chopped fresh herbs	1 tablespoon chopped fresh herbs
1 egg	1 egg
150 ml milk	¼ pint milk

Sift the flour, salt and pepper into a large mixing bowl and rub in the butter until the mixture is like fine breadcrumbs. Stir in the cheese and herbs. Beat the egg and milk together and stir into the dry ingredients. Mix to a stiff batter and put into a greased 0·5-kg/1-lb loaf tin. Bake in a moderately hot oven (190°C, 375°F, Gas Mark 5) for 45 minutes. Turn out to cool on a wire rack. Serve sliced and buttered.

Below: Cheese and Herb Bread; bottom: Summer Vegetable Quiche

Preserves

Spiced Redcurrant Jelly

This is a variation on the traditional redcurrant jelly, and it goes very well with roast lamb or with game. This jelly, which is also delicious served as a spread, will keep throughout the year in a sealed jar.

METRIC	IMPERIAL
1·5 kg redcurrants	3 lb redcurrants
600 ml water	1 pint water
150 ml white vinegar	$\frac{1}{4}$ pint white vinegar
3 cloves	3 cloves
$\frac{1}{2}$ cinnamon stick	$\frac{1}{2}$ cinnamon stick
sugar	sugar

Strip the redcurrants from their stems and put into a preserving pan with the water and vinegar. Put the cloves and cinnamon in a piece of muslin or clean cotton, tie into a bag and suspend in the liquid. Simmer until the fruit is very soft. Take out the spice bag. Strain the redcurrant liquid through a jelly bag or clean cloth, and measure the juice. Allow 450 g/1 lb sugar to each 600 ml/1 pint juice. Put the sugar and juice into a pan and heat gently, stirring until the sugar has dissolved. Boil hard for 5–10 minutes to setting point, when a little of the mixture dropped on a cold saucer will set quickly and wrinkle when pushed with a finger. Pour into small sterilised jars and cover.

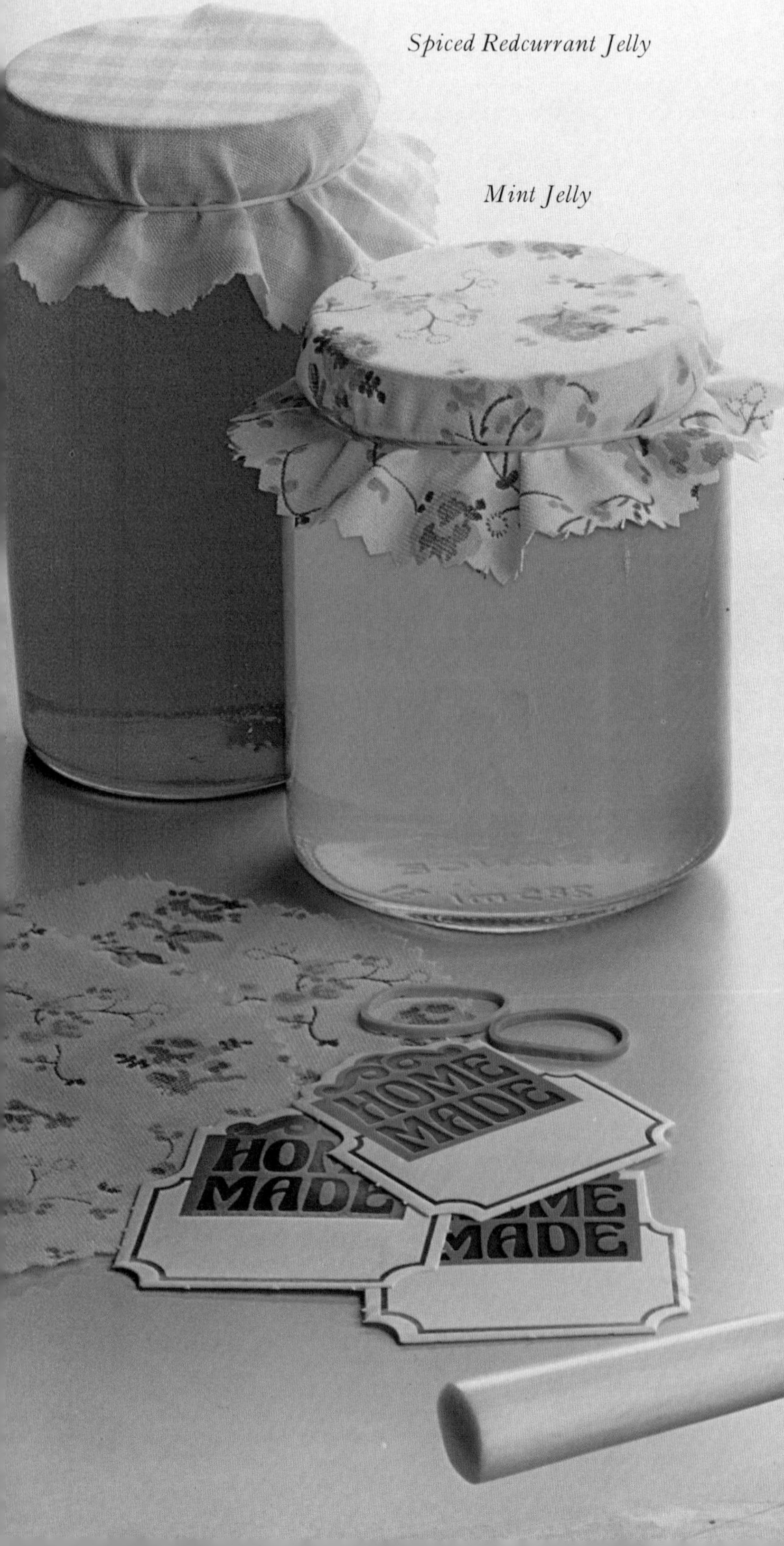

Spiced Redcurrant Jelly

Mint Jelly

Mint Jelly

This preserve may be made with apples, but it is a better colour when prepared with gooseberries. Put it into small jars to use with roast lamb.

METRIC	IMPERIAL
1·75 kg gooseberries	4 lb gooseberries
sugar	sugar
large bunch of fresh mint	large bunch of fresh mint
6 tablespoons finely chopped fresh mint	6 tablespoons finely chopped fresh mint

Top and tail the gooseberries and put them into a pan with just enough water to cover. Simmer until the fruit is soft and broken. Strain through a jelly bag or clean cloth, and measure the liquid. Allow 450 g/1 lb sugar to each 600 ml/1 pint of juice. Stir the sugar into the juice over a low heat until the sugar has dissolved. Tie up the bunch of mint and suspend it in the pan. Boil hard to setting point, when a little of the mixture dropped on a cold saucer will set quickly and wrinkle when pushed with a finger. Lift out the bunch of mint. Stir the chopped mint into the pan and simmer for 1 minute. Pour into small warmed, sterilised jars and cover.

Summer Four-Fruit Jam

This is an unusual jam which makes the best of very little fruit, and which can be prepared at the end of the soft fruit season. It is very good on toast or biscuits, or may be used as a cake filling.

METRIC	IMPERIAL
225 g blackcurrants	8 oz blackcurrants
225 g redcurrants	8 oz redcurrants
150 ml water	$\frac{1}{4}$ pint water
225 g raspberries	8 oz raspberries
225 g strawberries	8 oz strawberries
900 g sugar	2 lb sugar

Remove the blackcurrants and redcurrants from their stems. Put the blackcurrants in a pan with the water and simmer for 10 minutes until tender. Add the other fruit and simmer for 10 minutes, stirring occasionally. Stir in the sugar over a low heat until dissolved, then boil hard to setting point, when a little of the mixture dropped on a cold saucer will set quickly and wrinkle when pushed with a finger. Pour into warmed sterilised jars and cover.

Summer Four-Fruit Jam

August

This is holiday month so everyone needs food which can be eaten easily for picnics and light suppers. The summer fruit and vegetables are coming to an end, but there are huge supplies of home-grown and imported fruit for eating and preserving.

Foods in Season

FISH

Brill · Carp · Crab · Crayfish · Haddock · Hake · Halibut · Herring · Lobster · Mullet · Pike
Plaice · Prawns · Salmon · Salmon trout · Sole · Trout · Turbot

POULTRY AND GAME

Chicken · Duck · Grouse · Hare · Venison

VEGETABLES
(home produced and imported)

Aubergines · Cabbage · Cauliflower · Corn-on-the-cob · Courgettes · French beans
Globe artichokes · Marrows · Peas · Peppers · Runner beans · Spinach · Tomatoes

FRUIT
(home produced and imported)

Apples · Blackberries · Damsons · Figs · Greengages · Melons · Peaches · Pears · Plums

Freezer Notes

While summer vegetables are coming to an end, there is a profusion of autumn ones to be preserved. Runner beans, corn-on-the-cob and tomatoes will all add variety to winter meals. Apples, pears, plums and blackberries may be frozen in sugar or in syrup, or can be made into pies or puddings. For those who like game, the season opens for grouse and hare.

Soups and Starters

Sweet Corn Chowder

The sweet corn kernels for this soup may be frozen or canned, or they may be scraped from a freshly cooked cob. The soup is filling enough for a complete meal with some crusty bread, and is very welcome after a busy day in the open air.

METRIC	IMPERIAL
1 medium onion	1 medium onion
450 g potatoes	1 lb potatoes
1·15 litres milk	2 pints milk
175 g sweet corn kernels	6 oz sweet corn kernels
225 g smoked haddock fillet	8 oz smoked haddock fillet
salt and pepper	salt and pepper
25 g butter	1 oz butter
1 tablespoon chopped parsley to garnish	1 tablespoon chopped parsley to garnish

Peel the onion and slice thinly. Peel the potatoes and cut them into 2·5-cm/1-inch cubes. Put the onion and potato into a pan with the milk and simmer for 15 minutes. Add the sweet corn kernels. Cut the fish into 2·5-cm/1-inch squares and add to the pan. Continue simmering for 10 minutes. Season to taste and stir in the butter. Pour into a tureen or individual bowls and garnish with parsley. Serves 4

Right: Tomato and Orange Soup; below: Sweet Corn Chowder

Tomato and Orange Soup

METRIC	IMPERIAL
1 kg ripe tomatoes	2 lb ripe tomatoes
1 medium onion, sliced	1 medium onion, sliced
1 medium carrot, sliced	1 medium carrot, sliced
grated rind of ½ lemon	grated rind of ½ lemon
1 bay leaf	1 bay leaf
salt and pepper	salt and pepper
½ teaspoon sugar	½ teaspoon sugar
1·15 litres chicken stock	2 pints chicken stock
40 g butter	1½ oz butter
40 g plain flour	1½ oz plain flour
1 orange	1 orange
150 ml single cream (optional)	¼ pint single cream (optional)

Chop the tomatoes, including the skins and pips. Put into a pan with the onion, carrot, lemon rind, bay leaf, salt, pepper, sugar and stock. Cover and simmer for 30 minutes until the tomatoes are soft, then sieve.

Melt the butter in a clean pan and stir in the flour. Cook and stir for 1 minute. Pour on the tomato liquid, stir well and bring to the boil. Peel the orange very thinly, and cut the peel into fine shreds. Put the peel into a small pan of boiling water, boil for 3 minutes, and then drain and reserve the peel. Squeeze the juice from the orange and add to the soup. Adjust the seasoning and simmer for 5 minutes. If using cream, stir it in just before serving, and garnish with the peel. Serve hot or chilled. Serves 4–6

Rabbit Pâté

Rabbit Pâté

METRIC	IMPERIAL
1 rabbit	1 rabbit
150 ml light ale	¼ pint light ale
225 g belly pork	8 oz belly pork
2 bay leaves	2 bay leaves
1 sprig thyme	1 sprig thyme
1 sprig parsley	1 sprig parsley
salt and pepper	salt and pepper
175 g streaky bacon rashers	6 oz streaky bacon rashers

Remove the flesh from the rabbit with a sharp knife and cut it into small pieces. Put into a bowl with the light ale. Cut the pork into small cubes and add to the bowl with the bay leaf, thyme, parsley and seasoning. Leave in a cold place for 8 hours.

Drain the meat, reserving the liquid. Mince the rabbit finely. Mince the pork coarsely. Remove the rind from the bacon and flatten the rashers out very thinly with a wide-bladed knife. Line a 1-kg/2-lb loaf tin or terrine with the rashers. Put in the pork and rabbit in layers. Strain the liquid and pour over the meat. Cover with a piece of kitchen foil and a lid and put the container into a roasting tin half filled with water. Cook in a cool oven (150°C, 300°F, Gas Mark 2) for 2 hours. Cool under weights for 24 hours. Slice and serve with salad or toast. Serves 8

Pork and Liver Pâté

METRIC	IMPERIAL
350 g pig's liver	12 oz pig's liver
1 kg belly pork, boned and skinned	2 lb belly pork, boned and skinned
1 large onion, chopped	1 large onion, chopped
25 g butter	1 oz butter
1 egg	1 egg
1 tablespoon plain flour	1 tablespoon plain flour
salt and pepper	salt and pepper
pinch of grated nutmeg	pinch of grated nutmeg
1 tablespoon chopped parsley	1 tablespoon chopped parsley
1 bay leaf	1 bay leaf
100 g streaky bacon, cut in thin rashers	4 oz streaky bacon, cut in thin rashers

Stuffed Tomatoes

METRIC	IMPERIAL
8 medium tomatoes	8 medium tomatoes
75 g full-fat soft cheese	3 oz full-fat soft cheese
2 eggs, hard-boiled	2 eggs, hard-boiled
1 small onion, grated	1 small onion, grated
½ green pepper, chopped	½ green pepper, chopped
2 teaspoons salad cream	2 teaspoons salad cream
salt and pepper	salt and pepper
75 g peeled prawns	3 oz peeled prawns
lettuce leaves to garnish	lettuce leaves to garnish

Cut out a small slice from the top of each tomato. Scoop out the core and seeds from each one with a spoon. Put the cheese into a bowl and cream with a fork until smooth. Chop the eggs finely. Mix the eggs, onion, green pepper, salad cream, salt and pepper with the cheese. Reserve some prawns for garnish.

Chop the remaining prawns in quarters and fold into the cheese mixture. Fill the tomatoes with the cheese mixture and garnish each one with prawns. Arrange on a bed of lettuce leaves. Serves 4

Note These tomatoes also make a delicious salad accompaniment.

Above left: Pork and Liver Pâté;
below: Stuffed Tomatoes

Mince the liver and pork coarsely. Soften the onion in the butter until just golden. Put the meat, onion and cooking juices, egg, flour, seasoning, nutmeg and parsley into a liquidiser and blend at maximum speed for 5 minutes (in a small goblet, it may be necessary to process the meat in small quantities).

Put the bay leaf on the base of a 1-kg/2-lb loaf tin or terrine. Stretch the bacon out as thinly as possible with a wide-bladed knife. Line the container with the bacon. Put in the meat mixture and cover with greaseproof paper and a lid. Stand the container in a roasting tin half filled with water and cook in a moderate oven (180°C, 350°F, Gas Mark 4) for 1¾ hours. Cool under weights for 24 hours. Turn out and serve in slices with salad or toast. Serves 12

Melon with Curried Cream and Prawns

Melon with Curried Cream and Prawns

A very ripe, sweet melon should be used for this delicious starter. It provides a contrast with the spiced richness of the cream and the fresh taste and firm texture of the prawns.

METRIC	IMPERIAL
1 medium honeydew melon	1 medium honeydew melon
300 ml double cream	½ pint double cream
2 teaspoons mild curry powder	2 teaspoons mild curry powder
squeeze of lemon juice	squeeze of lemon juice
175 g peeled prawns	6 oz peeled prawns

Cut the melon into four or six even-sized wedges. Whip the cream to soft peaks and mix in curry powder and lemon juice until the cream is just lightly coloured. Put the melon slices on a serving plate and top each with a generous portion of whipped cream. Garnish generously with prawns. Serve chilled. Serves 4–6

Seafood Dip

Seafood Dip

The fish for this dip may be fresh, frozen or canned. It has a delicious flavour for a summer party, and is best served with crisps or small biscuits for dipping.

METRIC	IMPERIAL
225 g crabmeat	8 oz crabmeat
225 g full-fat soft cheese	8 oz full-fat soft cheese
1 (142-ml) carton natural yogurt	1 (5-fl oz) carton natural yogurt
1 tablespoon tomato ketchup	1 tablespoon tomato ketchup
1 tablespoon lemon juice	1 tablespoon lemon juice
salt and pepper	salt and pepper
100 g peeled shrimps or prawns	4 oz peeled shrimps or prawns
few unpeeled prawns to garnish	few unpeeled prawns to garnish

Put the crabmeat, cheese, yogurt, tomato ketchup and lemon juice into a liquidiser and blend until smooth. Season to taste. Chop the shrimps or prawns into six or eight pieces, leaving a few whole, and stir into the mixture. Put into a serving dish and garnish with the whole and unpeeled prawns. Chill before serving. Serves **8**

Main Dishes

Bacon Pasties

METRIC	IMPERIAL
350 g shortcrust pastry	12 oz shortcrust pastry
225 g lean steak, minced	8 oz lean steak, minced
2 lamb's kidneys, chopped	2 lamb's kidneys, chopped
100 g streaky bacon, chopped	4 oz streaky bacon, chopped
1 medium onion, chopped	1 medium onion, chopped
salt and pepper	salt and pepper
1 teaspoon Worcestershire sauce	1 teaspoon Worcestershire sauce
beaten egg to glaze	beaten egg to glaze

Roll out the pastry and cut into six 18-cm/7-inch rounds. Mix the steak, kidney, bacon and onion together and season with salt, pepper and sauce. Put a sixth of the mixture on half of each round. Fold over the edges to form half-moon shapes and flute the edges with the fingers to make the edging. Make leaf shapes from the pastry trimmings and use as a decoration. Brush well with the egg. Bake in a hot oven (220°C, 425°F, Gas Mark 7) for 15 minutes. Reduce the heat to moderate (180°C, 350°F, Gas Mark 4) for 45 minutes. Serve hot or cold. Serves 6

Devilled Poacher's Roll

METRIC	IMPERIAL
350 g frozen puff pastry	12 oz frozen puff pastry
175 g streaky bacon	6 oz streaky bacon
1 small onion, chopped	1 small onion, chopped
50 g button mushrooms, chopped	2 oz button mushrooms, chopped
450 g pork sausagemeat	1 lb pork sausagemeat
1 tablespoon French mustard	1 tablespoon French mustard
1 tablespoon dried mixed herbs	1 tablespoon dried mixed herbs
salt and pepper	salt and pepper
1 tablespoon sweet chutney	1 tablespoon sweet chutney
beaten egg to glaze	beaten egg to glaze

Roll out the pastry to a 30 × 25-cm/12 × 18-inch oblong Chop the bacon and mix with the onion, mushrooms, sausagemeat, mustard, herbs, salt and pepper. Spread the pastry with the chutney. Form the meat mixture into a sausage shape and place in the centre of the pastry. Pull up the edges of the pastry to enclose the meat completely. Place on a baking tray with the join underneath. Decorate the top with any pastry trimmings and make three slashes on the top, cutting diagonally. Brush with the egg, beaten with a pinch of salt. Bake in a hot oven (220°C, 425°F, Gas Mark 7) for 20 minutes. Reduce the oven to moderately hot (190°C, 375°F, Gas Mark 5) for 40 minutes. Serve hot or cold. Serves 6

Pissaladière

This favourite dish from the South of France is made on a base of bread dough, or on thick slices of bread fried in olive oil. It may also be made with an unsweetened scone dough, but this version with a pastry base is particularly good for a picnic as it is less heavy when eaten cold.

METRIC	IMPERIAL
200 g plain flour	7 oz plain flour
50 g butter	2 oz butter
40 g lard	1½ oz lard
pinch of salt	pinch of salt
150 ml olive oil	¼ pint olive oil
900 g onions, sliced	2 lb onions, sliced
100 g black olives, stoned	4 oz black olives, stoned
75 g canned anchovy fillets	3 oz canned anchovy fillets

Sift the flour into a bowl and rub in the butter and lard with the salt until the mixture is like fine breadcrumbs. Work in just enough cold water to make a firm dough. Roll out to fit an 18 × 28-cm/7 × 11-inch oblong tin.

Put the oil into a pan and heat. Add the onions and let them cook very slowly without browning for 45 minutes. They should be very soft indeed. Put the onions on to the pastry. Arrange the olives and anchovies in a lattice on top. Bake in a moderately hot oven (200°C, 400°F, Gas Mark 6) for 35 minutes. Serve very hot, cut in squares, or cool to take on a picnic. Serves 6–8

Sweet Things

Apricot Custard Tart

METRIC	IMPERIAL
225 g shortcrust pastry	8 oz shortcrust pastry
8 ripe apricots	8 ripe apricots
3 eggs	3 eggs
15 g cornflour	$\frac{1}{2}$ oz cornflour
300 ml creamy milk	$\frac{1}{2}$ pint creamy milk
100 g sugar	4 oz sugar
few drops of vanilla essence	few drops of vanilla essence

Line a 20-cm/8-inch flan ring with the pastry and bake blind in a moderately hot oven (200°C, 400°F, Gas Mark 6) for 15 minutes. Peel the apricots, cut them in half and take out the stones. Arrange the fruit cut side down on the pastry.

Break the eggs into a bowl and whisk them. Mix the cornflour with a little of the milk. Heat the sugar and milk together just to boiling point. Beat into the eggs and stir in the cornflour mixture. Return to the pan and stir gently over a low heat until the custard is creamy. Flavour lightly with vanilla. Cool to lukewarm, stirring occasionally. Pour over the apricots. Bake in a moderate oven (190°C, 375°F, Gas Mark 5) for 35 minutes. Serves 6

Picnic Fruit Cake

METRIC	IMPERIAL
225 g mixed dried fruit	8 oz mixed dried fruit
100 g sugar	4 oz sugar
150 ml warm tea without milk	$\frac{1}{4}$ pint warm tea without milk
1 egg	1 egg
2 tablespoons marmalade	2 tablespoons marmalade
275 g self-raising flour	10 oz self-raising flour

Put the fruit into a bowl with the sugar. Pour on the tea and leave to stand for 8 hours. Stir the egg and marmalade into the bowl. Add the flour and beat until well mixed. Put into a greased 0·5-kg/1-lb loaf tin. Bake in a moderate oven (160°C, 325°F, Gas Mark 3) for $1\frac{3}{4}$ hours. Cool in the tin for 15 minutes, and then turn out and finish cooling on a wire rack. Serve with butter if liked.

Apricot Custard Tart

Baking

Flowerpot Bread

Long before tins were used, bread was baked in clay pots which retained the loaves' rich flavour. Today, small flowerpots not only impart a special taste, but give an attractively shaped loaf to eat with cheese or salad. Try to use new pots for baking, and keep them clean for re-use. Grease new pots well with lard or oil and bake them empty in a hot oven once or twice before use. This recipe is enough for two 13-cm/5-inch pots.

METRIC	IMPERIAL
175 g strong plain white flour	6 oz strong plain white flour
225 g wholemeal flour	8 oz wholemeal flour
2 teaspoons salt	2 teaspoons salt
15 g lard	½ oz lard
2 teaspoons castor sugar	2 teaspoons castor sugar
15 g fresh yeast	½ oz fresh yeast
300 ml lukewarm water	½ pint lukewarm water

Stir the white and wholemeal flours with the salt in a bowl. Rub in the lard and mix in the sugar. Cream the yeast with a little of the lukewarm water, and add the remaining water. Stir into the flour and mix to a soft scone-like dough which leaves the bowl clean. Knead the dough on a lightly floured board until smooth – this will take about 2 minutes.

Divide the dough in half and put into two well greased flowerpots. Put into a large, lightly oiled polythene bag, tied loosely at the top. Leave to rise in a warm place until the dough has doubled in size and springs back when pressed with a floured finger. Remove the bag. Put the pots of dough on to a baking tray, standing them upright. Bake in a hot oven (230°C, 450°F, Gas Mark 8) for 35 minutes. Turn out of the pots and leave to cool on a wire rack.

Picnic Fruit Cake

Wheatmeal Cheese Biscuits

METRIC	IMPERIAL
100 g wholemeal flour	4 oz wholemeal flour
pinch of salt	pinch of salt
pinch of cayenne pepper	pinch of cayenne pepper
1 teaspoon dry mustard	1 teaspoon dry mustard
25 g butter	1 oz butter
100 g Cheddar cheese, grated	4 oz Cheddar cheese, grated
2 tablespoons water	2 tablespoons water

Mix the flour, salt, cayenne and mustard together in a bowl. Rub in the butter and then stir in the cheese. Add the water and mix to a dough. Roll out thinly and cut into 5-cm/2-inch rounds.

Arrange on a greased baking tray and prick each biscuit four or five times with a fork. Bake in a hot oven (230°C, 450°F, Gas Mark 8) for 8 minutes. The biscuits should be puffed up and golden brown. Lift carefully on to a wire rack to cool.

Suffolk Rusks

These little golden biscuits keep well and they are very good with cheese, or with butter and jam.

METRIC	IMPERIAL
225 g self-raising flour	8 oz self-raising flour
75 g butter	3 oz butter
1 egg	1 egg
little milk	little milk

Sift the flour into a bowl. Rub in the butter until the mixture is like fine breadcrumbs. Beat the egg and work into the mixture with just enough milk to give a soft dough as for scones. Roll out to 1 cm/½ inch thick and cut into 5-cm/2-inch rounds. Put on a baking tray close together and bake in a hot oven (230°C, 450°F, Gas Mark 8) for 10 minutes.

Remove from the oven and split in half with a sharp knife. Return to the baking tray with the cut side uppermost. Continue baking in a moderately hot oven (190°C, 375°F, Gas Mark 5) for 15 minutes until crisp and golden. Cool on a wire rack.

Below: Wheatmeal Cheese Biscuits;
below right: Suffolk Rusks

Peaches in Brandy Syrup

Preserves

Peaches in Brandy Syrup

When peaches are ripe and cheap, it is worth preserving some for winter use. Small peaches may be used, and make a delicious emergency pudding with cream in the winter.

METRIC	IMPERIAL
ripe peaches	ripe peaches
sugar	sugar
water	water
brandy	brandy

Weigh the peaches and for every 450 g/1 lb fruit, allow 350 g/12 oz sugar and 250 ml/8 fl oz water. Put the sugar and water into a large pan and stir over a low heat until the sugar has dissolved. Bring to the boil, and boil for 10 minutes without stirring.

While the syrup is cooking, dip the peaches in boiling water and rub off the skins. Add the fruit to the syrup and cook gently for about 5 minutes until tender. Lift the peaches from the syrup with a slotted spoon and pack firmly into hot sterilised preserving jars. Simmer the syrup for 5 minutes. Measure and add an equal quantity of brandy. Bring the syrup and brandy to boiling point and fill the jars of peaches to overflowing. Screw on the lids tightly.

September

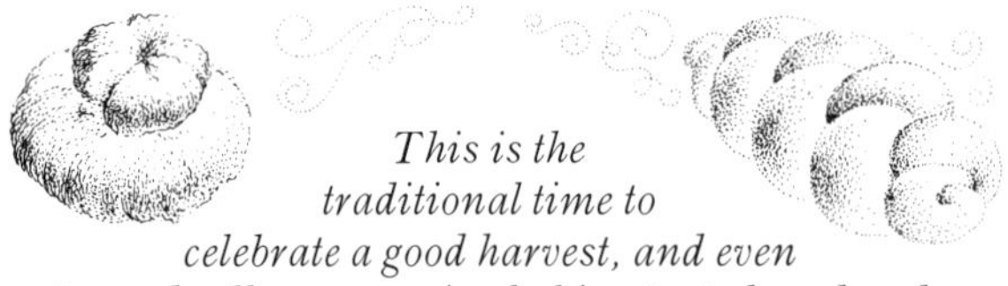

This is the traditional time to celebrate a good harvest, and even town-dwellers can enjoy baking tasty bread and preserving autumn bounty as jams and pickles. It is fun to go on a country expedition gathering apples and blackberries, or trying to find a supply of locally grown pears and plums.

Foods in Season

FISH

Carp · Crayfish · Dab · Haddock · Halibut · Herring · Lobster · Mullet · Mussels · Oysters
Pike · Plaice · Prawns · Sole · Trout

POULTRY AND GAME

Chicken · Duck · Goose · Turkey · Grouse · Hare · Partridge · Rabbit · Snipe · Venison
Wild duck

VEGETABLES
(home produced and imported)

Aubergines · Cabbage · Cauliflower · Celery · Corn-on-the-cob · Courgettes · Leeks
Marrows · Onions · Parsnips · Peppers · Runner beans · Spinach · Swedes · Tomatoes

FRUIT
(home produced and imported)

Apples · Blackberries · Damsons · Grapes · Lemons · Oranges · Peaches · Pears · Plums

Freezer Notes

There is still time to freeze the profusion of autumn fruit and vegetables, but some of the winter ones are now appearing. There are the first sprouts, leeks and onions, some celery, and the last of the corn-on-the-cob which should be frozen before it becomes starchy. At the end of the summer holidays, there may be fresh fish to bring back for the freezer, and there will be plenty of rabbits and hares.

Soups and Starters

Mushroom Soup

METRIC	IMPERIAL
225 g mushrooms	8 oz mushrooms
1·15 litres water	2 pints water
1 small onion, chopped	1 small onion, chopped
50 g butter	2 oz butter
40 g plain flour	1½ oz plain flour
150 ml milk	¼ pint milk
salt and pepper	salt and pepper
pinch of grated nutmeg	pinch of grated nutmeg
150 ml single cream	¼ pint single cream
chopped parsley to garnish	chopped parsley to garnish

Wipe the mushrooms, but do not peel them. Cut them in pieces and put into a pan with the water. Simmer for 15 minutes. Cook the onion in the butter for 3 minutes until soft and golden. Work in the flour and cook for 1 minute. Add the mushrooms and cooking liquid, milk, salt and pepper. Cover and simmer for 15 minutes.

Put through a sieve or purée in a liquidiser. Add the nutmeg and reheat. Remove from the heat and stir in the cream. Reheat very gently without boiling. Serve garnished with parsley. Serves 4

Egg and Prawn Mousse

This makes a very good first course, but it is also suitable for a light meal if served with salad.

METRIC	IMPERIAL
6 eggs, hard-boiled	6 eggs, hard-boiled
250 ml mayonnaise	8 fl oz mayonnaise
2 teaspoons gelatine	2 teaspoons gelatine
4 tablespoons water	4 tablespoons water
pinch of cayenne pepper	pinch of cayenne pepper
3 drops of Tabasco sauce	3 drops of Tabasco sauce
4½ tablespoons double cream	4½ tablespoons double cream
Topping	*Topping*
4 tablespoons mayonnaise	4 tablespoons mayonnaise
3 tablespoons tomato ketchup (optional)	3 tablespoons tomato ketchup (optional)
100 g peeled prawns	4 oz peeled prawns
twist of lemon	twist of lemon
parsley to garnish	parsley to garnish

Chop the eggs very finely by hand or in a liquidiser. Mix into the mayonnaise. Put the gelatine and water in a small bowl and stand this in a pan of hot water. Put over a low heat and stir until the gelatine is syrupy. Cool for 3 minutes, then stir into the egg mixture and add the cayenne and Tabasco. Whip the cream to soft peaks and fold into the mixture. Turn into a 15-cm/6-inch soufflé dish or other dish with straight sides. Put into the refrigerator and chill for 2 hours.

Mix the mayonnaise and tomato ketchup together until evenly coloured. Stir in the prawns. Spoon on top of the mousse just before serving. Serves 4

Main Dishes

Pigeon Casserole

METRIC	IMPERIAL
2 pigeons	2 pigeons
225 g stewing steak	8 oz stewing steak
2 rashers lean bacon	2 rashers lean bacon
25 g butter	1 oz butter
50 g button mushrooms	2 oz button mushrooms
300 ml beef stock	½ pint beef stock
salt and pepper	salt and pepper
1 tablespoon redcurrant jelly	1 tablespoon redcurrant jelly
1 tablespoon lemon juice	1 tablespoon lemon juice
15 g cornflour	½ oz cornflour

Wipe the pigeons and split them in half through the backbone. Cut the steak into cubes and the bacon into small pieces. Melt the butter and cook the pigeons and steak until just coloured. Wipe the mushrooms and add with the bacon, stock, salt and pepper. Put into a casserole, cover and cook in a moderate oven (160°C, 325°F, Gas Mark 3) for 1 hour.

Stir in the redcurrant jelly and lemon juice. Mix the cornflour with a little water, and stir into the casserole. Cover and continue cooking for 30 minutes. Serve with jacket potatoes cooked in the same oven. Serves 4

Pigeon Casserole

Beef Hotpot

METRIC	IMPERIAL
900 g potatoes, sliced	2 lb potatoes, sliced
450 g onions, sliced	1 lb onions, sliced
450 g stewing steak, cubed	1 lb stewing steak, cubed
2 teaspoons dried mixed herbs	2 teaspoons dried mixed herbs
2 bay leaves	2 bay leaves
600 ml beef stock	1 pint beef stock
salt and pepper	salt and pepper

Arrange layers of potatoes, onions and steak in a 1·25-litre/2-pint casserole, sprinkling each layer with herbs and seasoning. Insert the bay leaves halfway up the layers. Finish with a layer of potato. Pour on the stock. Cover and cook in a moderate oven (180°C, 350°F, Gas Mark 4) for $1\frac{1}{4}$ hours. Remove the lid and continue cooking for 15 minutes so that the potatoes become lightly browned. Serves 4

Beef-Stuffed Onions

This is a good way of using left-over meat from a joint to make a good lunch or supper dish. Use really large onions so that there is plenty of room for the stuffing.

METRIC	IMPERIAL
4 large onions	4 large onions
225 g cooked beef, minced	8 oz cooked beef, minced
50 g fresh breadcrumbs	2 oz fresh breadcrumbs
150 ml thick gravy	$\frac{1}{4}$ pint thick gravy
1 teaspoon tomato ketchup	1 teaspoon tomato ketchup
salt and pepper	salt and pepper
parsley to garnish	parsley to garnish

Peel the onions and put them in a pan with water to cover. Bring to the boil, and then simmer until the onions are tender but not broken. Drain off the water. Use a pointed knife to scoop the centres out of the onions into a bowl. Chop this scooped out flesh finely and mix with the meat. Reserve a few breadcrumbs for topping, and mix the rest into the meat with the gravy, tomato ketchup, salt and pepper. Put this filling into the onions.

Place the onions in a greased ovenproof dish and sprinkle the breadcrumbs on top. Put about 1 teaspoon oil or dripping on each onion. Bake in a moderately hot oven (200°C, 400°F, Gas Mark 6) for 45 minutes. Serve at once with some extra gravy if liked. Serves 4

Beef Hotpot

Beef-Stuffed Onions

Pork Pie

This traditional pie is made with hot water pastry which should be used while just warm as it has to be moulded, not rolled out.

METRIC	IMPERIAL
350 g plain flour	12 oz plain flour
1 teaspoon salt	1 teaspoon salt
150 g lard	5 oz lard
150 ml milk and water, mixed	¼ pint milk and water, mixed
900 g shoulder pork	2 lb shoulder pork
1 teaspoon chopped fresh sage	1 teaspoon chopped fresh sage
salt and pepper	salt and pepper
pinch of grated nutmeg	pinch of grated nutmeg
1 egg, beaten to glaze	1 egg, beaten to glaze
2·25 litres water	4 pints water
2 pig's trotters	2 pig's trotters
1 carrot	1 carrot
1 onion	1 onion
bunch of fresh mixed herbs	bunch of fresh mixed herbs

Sift the flour and salt into a warm bowl. Put the lard, milk and water into a pan and heat until the fat melts. Bring to the boil and pour at once into the centre of the flour. Using a wooden spoon, form into a paste. Turn on to a floured board and knead quickly until smooth. Cut off a third for the lid and decorations, cover and keep warm. Mould the remaining pastry to line the base and sides of an 18-cm/7-inch round cake tin with a removable base. The pastry should be of even thickness and free of cracks and should be moulded to come just above the edge of the tin.

Cut the meat into small dice and mix with the sage, salt, pepper and nutmeg. Press down into the pastry case and moisten with 3 tablespoons water. Roll out the remaining pastry to make a lid. Put on top of the meat and seal the edges. Make a small hole in the top with a skewer. Use the pastry trimmings to make leaves to decorate the top. Brush thickly with the egg, beaten with a pinch of salt. Bake in a hot oven (220°C, 425°F, Gas Mark 7) for 30 minutes. Reduce the heat to moderate (160°C, 325°F, Gas Mark 3) for 1½ hours. Cover the pie with a piece of greaseproof paper if it is getting too brown.

Meanwhile, put any meat trimmings into a pan with the water, trotters, carrot, onion, herbs and plenty of pepper. Bring to the boil, then cover and simmer for 3 hours. Strain and boil hard to reduce the stock to 450 ml/¾ pint. Season with salt and pepper to taste. Cool until the stock is syrupy, like half-set jelly. If liked, this stock may be prepared beforehand and cooled in the refrigerator.

Take the pie from the oven, but leave it in the tin. Leave to cool for 1½ hours, then use a small funnel, or one made from a piece of kitchen foil, and gently spoon in the cool stock. This may need to be repeated two or three times as the stock will sink into the meat as it cools. Leave in a cold place for 8 hours before removing from the tin. Serves 6–8

Pork Pie

Sweet Things

Eve's Pudding

METRIC	IMPERIAL
225 g fresh breadcrumbs	8 oz fresh breadcrumbs
225 g shredded suet	8 oz shredded suet
225 g apples	8 oz apples
225 g currants	8 oz currants
50 g sugar	2 oz sugar
pinch of grated nutmeg	pinch of grated nutmeg
3 eggs	3 eggs

Stir the breadcrumbs and shredded suet together. Peel and core the apples and chop the flesh into small dice. Add to the dry ingredients the currants, sugar and nutmeg. Beat the eggs lightly and stir into the mixture. Beat together until well mixed.

Turn into a greased 1·25-litre/2-pint pudding basin and cover securely with greaseproof paper and kitchen foil. Stand in a pan with boiling water to come halfway up the sides of the basin. Cover and boil for 2 hours, adding more boiling water occasionally. Turn out on to a hot serving dish and serve with custard, warm golden syrup or apricot jam. Serves 6

Essex Plum Sponge

Essex Plum Sponge

The perfect plums for this pudding are the small dark plums which used to be grown everywhere in Essex, but any ripe sweet ones will do. Serve the sponge with custard, cream or ice cream.

METRIC	IMPERIAL
450 g plums	1 lb plums
50 g sugar	2 oz sugar
2 tablespoons water	2 tablespoons water
Sponge	*Sponge*
100 g butter	4 oz butter
100 g castor sugar	4 oz castor sugar
2 eggs	2 eggs
100 g self-raising flour	4 oz self-raising flour
Topping	*Topping*
50 g plain flour	2 oz plain flour
1 teaspoon ground mixed spice	1 teaspoon ground mixed spice
25 g butter	1 oz butter
50 g demerara sugar	2 oz demerara sugar
25 g hazelnuts, chopped	1 oz hazelnuts, chopped
2 tablespoons plum jam	2 tablespoons plum jam

Cut the plums in half and remove the stones. Put into a 1·5-litre/2½-pint ovenproof dish and stir in the sugar and water. Cream the butter and castor sugar until light and fluffy. Work in the eggs and then the flour. Beat until creamy. Spread over the plums and bake in a moderately hot oven (190°C, 375°F, Gas Mark 5) for 35 minutes.

To prepare the topping, stir the flour and spice together and rub in the butter. Stir in the demerara sugar and nuts. Spread the jam evenly over the cooked sponge and sprinkle on the topping. Return to the oven for 15 minutes until the topping is golden. Serves 4–6

Eve's Pudding

Apple Ice with Sultana Sauce

METRIC	IMPERIAL
675 g cooking apples	$1\frac{1}{2}$ lb cooking apples
175 g castor sugar	6 oz castor sugar
2 lemons	2 lemons
$\frac{1}{4}$ teaspoon ground cinnamon	$\frac{1}{4}$ teaspoon ground cinnamon
600 ml water	1 pint water
few drops of green vegetable colouring	few drops of green vegetable colouring
3 tablespoons brandy	3 tablespoons brandy
150 ml double cream	$\frac{1}{4}$ pint double cream
Sauce	*Sauce*
225 g sultanas	8 oz sultanas
300 ml water	$\frac{1}{2}$ pint water
2 tablespoons light rum	2 tablespoons light rum
75 g castor sugar	3 oz castor sugar
1 bay leaf	1 bay leaf

Peel the apples, remove the cores, and cut into thin slices. Put into a pan with the sugar and the thinly sliced rind of 1 lemon. Add the cinnamon and water. Simmer until the apples are tender. Squeeze the juice from both lemons and add to the apples. Put through a sieve and then colour lightly to make a pale green purée. Stir in the brandy and cool. Put into an ice-making tray and freeze at the lowest setting of the refrigerator for $1\frac{1}{2}$ hours, until the mixture is like a thick batter. Whip the cream to soft peaks, and fold into the apple mixture. Freeze for $1\frac{1}{2}$ hours.

Put the sultanas, water, rum, sugar and bay leaf into a pan. Add the peel from the second lemon. Simmer until the mixture is like thick cream. Take out the bay leaf and lemon peel, and chill the sauce. Spoon the apple ice into four individual dishes and top with the sauce. Serves 4

Pear and Cider Compote

Cooking pears may be used, or hard dessert pears, as they will soften during long slow cooking. Red wine may be substituted for the cider.

METRIC	IMPERIAL
1 kg cooking pears	2 lb cooking pears
100 g castor sugar	4 oz castor sugar
300 ml dry cider	$\frac{1}{2}$ pint dry cider
300 ml water	$\frac{1}{2}$ pint water
strip of lemon rind	strip of lemon rind
50 g blanched almonds, shredded	2 oz blanched almonds, shredded

Below: Apple Ice with Sultana Sauce; right: Pear and Cider Compote

Peel the pears but leave them whole, with the stems on. Arrange them upright in a deep casserole. Sprinkle on the sugar. Mix the cider and water and pour over the pears. Add the lemon rind. Cover and bake in a cool oven (150°C, 300°F, Gas Mark 2) for 3 hours. Test the pears for softness by piercing them with a fork, and cook a little longer if they are not tender. Leave in the juice until lukewarm.

Lift the pears out with a slotted spoon and arrange them in a serving dish. Put the cooking liquid into a saucepan and simmer until thick and syrupy. Pour over the pears. Stick the almonds all over the pears. Chill, then serve with cream. Serves 6

Blackberry Cake

This cake can be served as a teatime treat or as a dessert with cream.

METRIC	IMPERIAL
100 g butter	4 oz butter
100 g sugar	4 oz sugar
1 egg	1 egg
225 g plain flour	8 oz plain flour
2 teaspoons baking powder	2 teaspoons baking powder
pinch of salt	pinch of salt
150 ml milk	$\frac{1}{4}$ pint milk
Topping	*Topping*
225 g ripe blackberries	8 oz ripe blackberries
50 g butter	2 oz butter
100 g light soft brown sugar	4 oz light soft brown sugar
50 g plain flour	2 oz plain flour
$\frac{1}{2}$ teaspoon ground mixed spice	$\frac{1}{2}$ teaspoon ground mixed spice

Cream the butter and sugar and beat in the egg. Sift the flour with the baking powder and salt. Add to the creamed mixture with the milk and beat to a smooth batter. Grease an 18 × 28-cm/7 × 11-inch tin. Pour in the cake mixture and sprinkle thickly with the blackberries.

Cream the butter and sugar. Work in the flour and spice to a crumble consistency and sprinkle over the blackberries. Bake in a moderate oven (180°C, 350°F, Gas Mark 4) for 1 hour. Cool in the tin and cut into squares to serve.

If liked, some extra blackberries can be placed on top of the crumble mixture prior to baking.

Blackberry Cake

Harvest Loaf

Malt Loaf

Baking

Malt Loaf

This is an easy cake-bread which can be made without yeast. It is very good sliced thickly and spread with butter or cream cheese.

METRIC	IMPERIAL
75 g malt extract	3 oz malt extract
50 g dark soft brown sugar	2 oz dark soft brown sugar
25 g butter	1 oz butter
150 ml milk and water mixed	¼ pint milk and water mixed
225 g wholemeal flour	8 oz wholemeal flour
2 teaspoons baking powder	2 teaspoons baking powder
¼ teaspoon salt	¼ teaspoon salt
25 g currants	1 oz currants
25 g sultanas	1 oz sultanas
50 g mixed nuts, chopped	2 oz mixed nuts, chopped

Put the malt extract, sugar, butter and liquid into a pan and heat gently until the fat has melted. Cool until lukewarm. Stir the flour, baking powder and salt together in a bowl and pour in the malt mixture. Beat well and add the currants, sultanas and nuts. Mix thoroughly and put into a greased 0·5-kg/1-lb loaf tin. Bake in a moderate oven (160°C, 325°F, Gas Mark 3) for 1½ hours. Cool for 5 minutes, and turn out on to a wire rack to cool completely.

Harvest Loaf

This loaf is shaped like a sheaf of corn, complete with harvest mouse. It should be richly golden in colour, and may be used for a festival decoration in church. This recipe gives a simpler version of the one illustrated on page 129.

METRIC	IMPERIAL
1·5kg strong plain white flour	3 lb strong plain white flour
6 teaspoons salt	6 teaspoons salt
25 g fresh yeast	1 oz fresh yeast
900 ml lukewarm water	1½ pints lukewarm water
beaten egg to glaze	beaten egg to glaze
few drops of gravy browning	few drops of gravy browning
2 currants	2 currants

Before preparing the dough, arrange the baking trays on which the design will be modelled. Take a shelf from the oven and arrange two baking trays on it, touching each other, to make one large surface. Cover with a piece of kitchen foil.

Sift the flour and salt into a warm bowl. Mix the yeast with a little of the lukewarm water, and then mix with the remaining water. Pour into the flour and mix well to form a dough. Knead on a board until smooth, then put into a clean greased bowl. Cover with a damp cloth and leave in a warm place until double in bulk – about 1–1½ hours. The dough can then be shaped, and does not need a second proving.

1 · Take 225 g/8 oz of the dough and form into a sausage shape about 30 cm/12 inches long. Put in the centre of the baking trays and flatten slightly. This forms the base of the design.

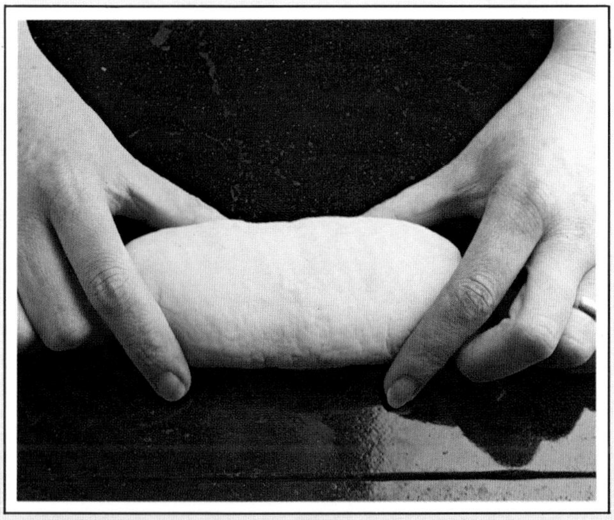

2 · Take 350 g/12 oz of the dough and form a crescent shape. Arrange this round the top of the flattened sausage shape and flatten with the hands.

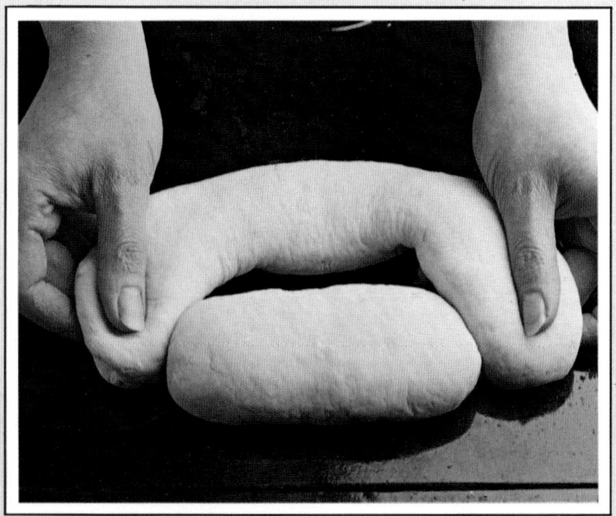

3 · Using half of the remaining dough, roll pieces with the hands into sticks a little thinner than a pencil and about 30 cm/12 inches long. Arrange along the basic sausage shape to cover it (these form the stalks of the corn). Make a plait with three of these pieces and put across the stalks, tucking the ends well under the base of the dough (this forms the tying string).

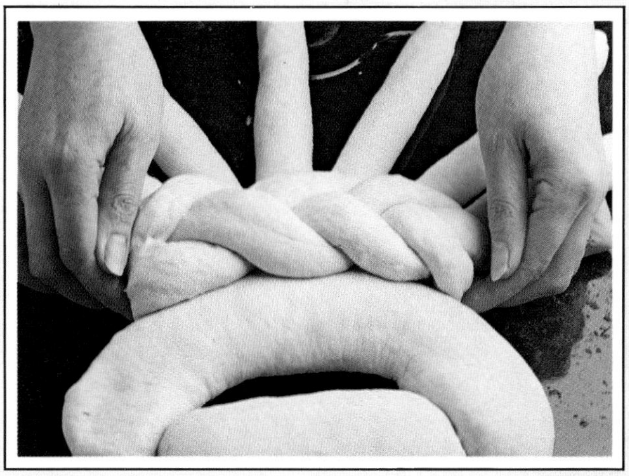

4 · Keep back 50 g/2 oz dough for the mouse. With the remaining dough, make small sausage shapes, about 25 g/1 oz each and arrange over the crescent like the rays of the sun (these form the ears of corn). Brush the whole sheaf thickly with the egg, beaten with a pinch of salt. Clip each sausage shape three or four times with a pair of scissors.

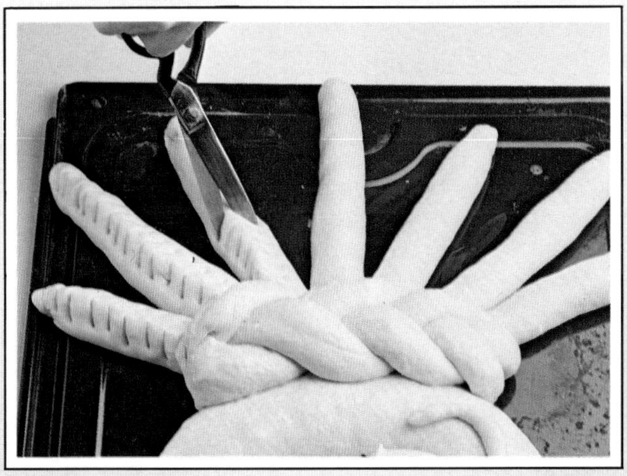

Knead a little gravy browning into the remaining dough, and shape it like a fat mouse with a long thin tail. Pinch the end of the dough to form a nose, and lift up small flaps for ears. Insert currants for eyes. Arrange the mouse on the 'stalks' and glaze with egg. Bake just above the centre of a hot oven (220°C, 425°F, Gas Mark 7) for 20 minutes. Lower the heat to moderate (160°C, 325°F, Gas Mark 3) and continue baking for 20 minutes. Leave on the baking tray until cold. Lift off carefully and peel away the foil.

Marrow Ginger Jam

Red Tomato Chutney

This richly coloured and flavoured chutney makes a welcome change from that made with green tomatoes. It is important to cook the chutney until it is of the consistency of thick jam, with all surplus liquid absorbed, as this gives a much more acceptable flavour and appearance.

METRIC	IMPERIAL
450 g ripe tomatoes	1 lb ripe tomatoes
100 g cooking apples	4 oz cooking apples
225 g onions, chopped	8 oz onions, chopped
450 g seedless raisins	1 lb seedless raisins
100 g dark soft brown sugar	4 oz dark soft brown sugar
2 teaspoons salt	2 teaspoons salt
3 teaspoons ground ginger	3 teaspoons ground ginger
pinch of cayenne pepper	pinch of cayenne pepper
300 ml vinegar	½ pint vinegar

Peel and chop the tomatoes. Peel and core the apples and chop them. Put the tomatoes, apples, onions and raisins into a pan with all the other ingredients. Bring to the boil, then simmer for at least 1¼ hours until thick and brown. Pour into sterilised jars and cover with waxed discs. Do not cover chutney with paper or it will dry out and shrink.

Preserves

Marrow Ginger Jam

METRIC	IMPERIAL
2·75 kg prepared marrow	6 lb prepared marrow
grated rind and juice of 4 lemons	grated rind and juice of 4 lemons
75 g root ginger	3 oz root ginger
2·75 kg sugar	6 lb sugar

Peel the marrow, and remove the seeds. Cut the flesh into cubes and then weigh the marrow. Put the marrow into a steamer and steam until just tender but not broken. Put into a large bowl. Add the lemon rind and juice to the marrow in the bowl. Put the ginger into a piece of muslin or clean cotton and beat it with a hammer to crush it into fibres. Tie the cloth into a bag and put it into the bowl with the sugar.

Leave to stand in a cool place for 24 hours. Put the contents of the bowl into a large pan and heat gently until the sugar has dissolved. Raise the heat and boil until the marrow is transparent and the syrup is thick. Remove the bag of ginger. Stir the preserve well, pour into hot sterilised jars and cover.

Red Tomato Chutney

Mild Piccalilli

Break the cauliflower into small pieces. Do not peel the marrow, but cut into cubes. Peel the onions or shallots. Cut the beans and celery into chunks. Do not peel the cucumber, but cut it into cubes. Mix the vegetables in a large bowl in layers with the salt. Cover with a plate to press down the vegetables so that they remain covered with salt. Leave for 24 hours.

Rinse the vegetables in fresh water and drain well. Mix the turmeric, mustard, ginger and sugar with all but 3 tablespoons of the vinegar. Put this mixture into a pan with the vegetables. Bring to the boil and then simmer for 15 minutes. Lift the vegetables out with a slotted spoon and pack into hot sterilised jars. Mix the cornflour with the remaining vinegar and stir into the cooking liquid. Bring to the boil and boil for 3 minutes, stirring all the time. Pour over the vegetables, pressing them down slightly so that the sauce runs between the pieces. Cover with waxed discs.

Mild Piccalilli

This popular mustard pickle is very useful for using up the last vegetables from the garden. The proportions of the vegetables may be varied, or some may be omitted, but the total weight should be used.

METRIC	IMPERIAL
225 g cauliflower	8 oz cauliflower
225 g marrow	8 oz marrow
225 g pickling onions or shallots	8 oz pickling onions or shallots
225 g French beans	8 oz French beans
225 g celery	8 oz celery
225 g cucumber	8 oz cucumber
225 g cooking salt	8 oz cooking salt
2 teaspoons turmeric	2 teaspoons turmeric
2 teaspoons dry mustard	2 teaspoons dry mustard
2 teaspoons ground ginger	2 teaspoons ground ginger
100 g sugar	4 oz sugar
900 ml white vinegar	$1\frac{1}{2}$ pints white vinegar
25 g cornflour	1 oz cornflour

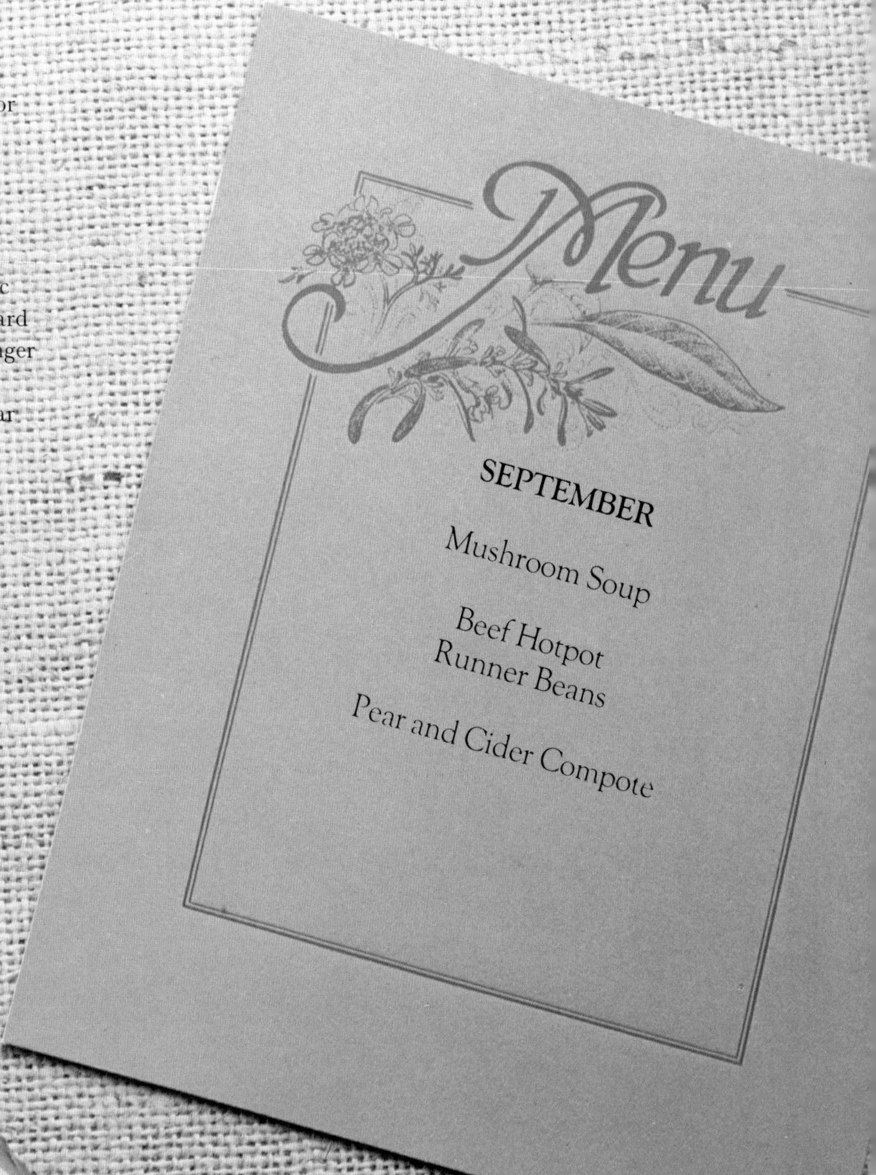

October

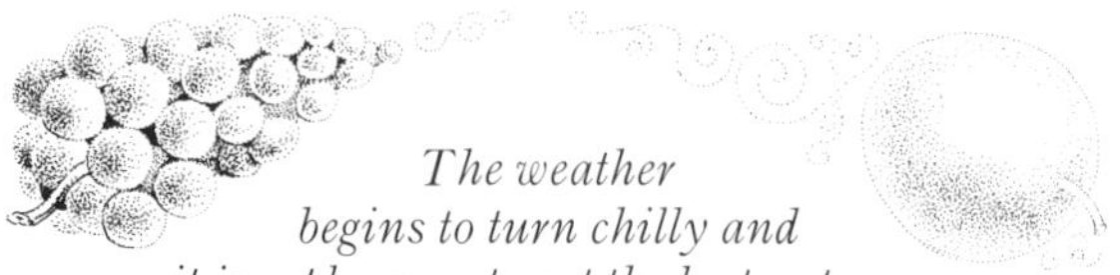

The weather begins to turn chilly and it is a pleasure to eat the last autumn foods by a warm fire. An old custom worth reviving is Hallowe'en (October 31st) when the witches ride and ghosts abound, and the children enjoy traditional apples and devil's food cake as they dress up and play crazy games.

Foods in Season

FISH

Carp · Cod · Dab · Haddock · Hake · Halibut · Herring · Lobster · Mackerel · Mussels Oysters · Pike · Plaice · Scallops · Skate · Sole

POULTRY AND GAME

Chicken · Duck · Goose · Turkey · Grouse · Hare · Partridge · Pheasant · Rabbit · Snipe Venison · Wild duck

VEGETABLES
(home produced and imported)

Broccoli · Brussels sprouts · Cabbage · Celery · Leeks · Marrows · Parsnips · Red cabbage Spinach · Swedes · Turnips

FRUIT
(home produced and imported)

Apples · Blackberries · Damsons · Grapes · Lemons · Oranges · Pears · Pomegranates Pumpkin · Quinces

Freezer Notes

This is a good time to make a bulk buy of beef or pork to provide plenty of winter meals, and pheasants are in season. Grapes and pears are worth freezing in syrup to add to fruit salads. It is worth cooking casseroles and pies for the freezer this month to leave plenty of time for Christmas shopping and food preparation.

Soups

Cauliflower Soup

METRIC	IMPERIAL
1 large cauliflower	1 large cauliflower
40 g butter	1½ oz butter
1 stick celery, chopped	1 stick celery, chopped
1 small leek, chopped	1 small leek, chopped
25 g ham, chopped	1 oz ham, chopped
1 bay leaf	1 bay leaf
600 ml chicken stock	1 pint chicken stock
300 ml milk	½ pint milk
salt and pepper	salt and pepper
4 tablespoons double cream	4 tablespoons double cream
25 g almonds, toasted	1 oz almonds, toasted

Clean the cauliflower and put into a pan. Cover with boiling salted water and cook until tender. Drain the cauliflower and break into pieces. Melt the butter and cook the celery, leek and ham for 5 minutes, stirring well. Add the bay leaf, cauliflower, stock and milk. Season and bring to the boil, then cover and simmer for 30 minutes. Put through a sieve or purée in a liquidiser. Reheat and adjust the seasoning. Just before serving, stir in the cream. Garnish with the toasted almonds. Serves 4

Oxtail and Sherry Soup

METRIC	IMPERIAL
1 oxtail, jointed	1 oxtail, jointed
1·4 litres water	2½ pints water
2 carrots, sliced	2 carrots, sliced
2 onions, sliced	2 onions, sliced
1 turnip, sliced	1 turnip, sliced
1 stick celery, sliced	1 stick celery, sliced
25 g seasoned flour	1 oz seasoned flour
½ teaspoon Worcestershire sauce	½ teaspoon Worcestershire sauce
2 tablespoons dry sherry	2 tablespoons dry sherry
1 tablespoon chopped parsley to garnish	1 tablespoon chopped parsley to garnish

Wipe the pieces of oxtail. Put into a pan and heat gently until the fat runs and the oxtail browns lightly. Put into a pan with the water and vegetables and bring to the boil. Cover and simmer for 2 hours. Remove the meat from the bones.

Put the meat, vegetables, cooking liquid and seasoned flour into a liquidiser and purée until smooth. Return to the pan with the Worcestershire sauce and simmer for 30 minutes. Adjust the seasoning, stir in the sherry and garnish with the parsley just before serving. Serves 4

Oxtail and Sherry Soup

Cauliflower Soup

Main Dishes

Savoury Stuffed Cod

METRIC	IMPERIAL
4 cod cutlets	4 cod cutlets
100 g fresh breadcrumbs	4 oz fresh breadcrumbs
1 tablespoon chopped parsley	1 tablespoon chopped parsley
½ teaspoon dried mixed herbs	½ teaspoon dried mixed herbs
salt and pepper	salt and pepper
grated rind and juice of ½ lemon	grated rind and juice of ½ lemon
1 egg	1 egg
50 g butter, melted	2 oz butter, melted
1 tomato	1 tomato
300 ml parsley sauce	½ pint parsley sauce

Remove the centre bone of each cutlet with a sharp knife. Arrange the cutlets in a greased ovenproof dish. Mix the crumbs with the parsley, mixed herbs, salt, pepper, lemon rind and juice and egg. Add half the butter and mix well. Pile this stuffing on the cod cutlets, pushing some down into the bone cavities. Peel the tomato and cut into eight slices. Arrange two slices on each piece of fish.

Pour on the remaining butter. Bake in a moderate oven (180°C, 350°F, Gas Mark 4) for 30 minutes. Serve with hot parsley sauce. Serves 4

Herrings in Oatmeal

METRIC	IMPERIAL
4 large herrings	4 large herrings
oil to baste	oil to baste
4 tablespoons porridge oats	4 tablespoons porridge oats
salt and pepper	salt and pepper

Wash the herrings and scrape off the scales, using a knife, from the tail towards the head. Trim off the fins and cut off the heads. Slit the fish down the belly and remove the roes and entrails. Press down hard on the fish to loosen the backbone, and remove the bones with the tail. Open out the fish completely.

Remove the rack from the grill pan and oil the pan lightly. Put the herrings in the pan, skin side downwards. Sprinkle with the oats, salt and pepper. Put the roes into the pan and season with salt and pepper. Sprinkle lightly with oil. Grill under medium heat for about 8 minutes. Arrange on a serving dish with the roes on top of the fish. Serve on their own for breakfast or a first course, or with boiled potatoes and peas as a main course. Serves 4

Beefburger Pasties

This is a simple way to make good use of a convenience food for a filling meal, good eaten hot with vegetables or cold for a picnic with salad.

METRIC	IMPERIAL
225 g shortcrust pastry	8 oz shortcrust pastry
4 beefburgers	4 beefburgers
1 medium onion, chopped	1 medium onion, chopped
1 tablespoon tomato ketchup	1 tablespoon tomato ketchup
4 large mushrooms	4 large mushrooms
beaten egg to glaze	beaten egg to glaze

Roll out the pastry thinly and cut out eight rounds slightly larger than the beefburgers. Place one beefburger on each of four rounds of pastry. Put a little chopped onion on each one with a teaspoon of ketchup. Put a mushroom on top of each one. Cover each beefburger with a second piece of pastry. Seal the edges well. Decorate with pastry leaves. Flute the edges and brush well with beaten egg. Bake in a hot oven (220°C, 425°F, Gas Mark 7) for 25 minutes. Serve hot or cold. Serves 4

Braised Beef

METRIC	IMPERIAL
450 g chuck steak	1 lb chuck steak
25 g dripping	1 oz dripping
1 teaspoon plain flour	1 teaspoon plain flour
1 teaspoon sugar	1 teaspoon sugar
salt and pepper	salt and pepper
1 teaspoon vinegar	1 teaspoon vinegar
2 teaspoons Worcestershire sauce	2 teaspoons Worcestershire sauce
150 ml water	$\frac{1}{4}$ pint water

Trim the excess fat from the meat and brown on both sides in the dripping. Drain off the surplus fat. Mix the flour, sugar and seasoning, and rub into both sides of the meat. Put into a 1-litre/$1\frac{1}{2}$-pint casserole and pour on the vinegar, sauce and water. Cover and cook in a moderate oven (160°C, 325°F, Gas Mark 3) for 2 hours. Serve with potatoes, baked in the same oven, and seasonal vegetables. Serves 4

Porky
Cider Casserole

Porky Cider Casserole

METRIC	IMPERIAL
4 pork chops	4 pork chops
1 medium onion, sliced	1 medium onion, sliced
1 teaspoon chopped fresh sage	1 teaspoon chopped fresh sage
salt and pepper	salt and pepper
150 ml stock	¼ pint stock
150 ml dry cider	¼ pint dry cider
1 cooking apple	1 cooking apple
2 tomatoes	2 tomatoes

Put the chops into a thick pan and put over low heat so that the fat runs. Cook until the chops are lightly browned on both sides. Add the onion and cook for 5 minutes. Drain off any surplus fat. Add the sage, salt, pepper, stock and cider. Cover and cook in a moderate oven (160°C, 325°F, Gas Mark 3) for 1 hour.

Peel the apple and tomatoes, cut out the apple cores and cut both across in slices. Arrange on top of the meat and continue cooking for a further 15 minutes. Remove the lid and cook for 10 minutes longer so that the top is golden. Serves 4

Pork and Liver Kebabs

Kebabs, or food cooked on a skewer, are not just for summer barbecues. They make very tasty autumn meals, served with boiled rice and a salad. Use long smooth kebab or turkey skewers, not the short variety.

METRIC	IMPERIAL
225 g lean pork	8 oz lean pork
50 g bacon rashers	2 oz bacon rashers
225 g liver	8 oz liver
2 dessert apples	2 dessert apples
4 bay leaves	4 bay leaves
salt and pepper	salt and pepper
2 teaspoons French mustard	2 teaspoons French mustard
olive oil to baste	olive oil to baste

Cut the pork into 2·5-cm/1-inch cubes. Cut the bacon in squares, and the liver into small pieces. Peel and core the apples and cut them into quarters. Thread the pork, bacon, liver and apple pieces on to four skewers, putting a bay leaf on each one about halfway along the skewer. Press the meat together firmly. Sprinkle lightly with salt and pepper and brush with the mustard. Brush lightly with olive oil. Grill under a medium heat for 12 minutes, turning the skewers often, and brushing with a little more oil to keep the meat moist. Serve at once with rice and salad. Serves 4

Below: Pork and Liver Kebabs;
bottom: Filled Jacket Potatoes

Filled Jacket Potatoes

Potatoes which are baked in their skins are delicious with butter and seasoning only, but they make complete meals if stuffed with cheese, flaked fish or meat.

METRIC	IMPERIAL
4 large potatoes	4 large potatoes
1 teaspoon salt	1 teaspoon salt
50 g butter, flaked	2 oz butter, flaked
100 g Cheddar cheese, grated	4 oz Cheddar cheese, grated
or 100 g cream cheese	or 4 oz cream cheese
or 225 g fish, cooked and flaked	or 8 oz fish, cooked and flaked
or 100 g bacon, cooked	or 4 oz bacon, cooked
parsley to garnish	parsley to garnish

Scrub the potatoes and rub them with the salt. Prick them well with a fork. Bake in a moderate oven (180°C, 350°F, Gas Mark 4) for $1\frac{1}{4}$ hours. Cut off the tops of the potatoes and scoop out about half the insides into a bowl. Beat in flakes of butter and season to taste. Add the chosen filling and mix lightly with the potatoes. Return to the potato skins. Put back in the oven with the tops in place, and continue cooking for 15 minutes. Garnish with parsley and serve with more butter and seasoning if liked. Serves 4

Sweet Things

Plum Upside-Down Pudding

METRIC	IMPERIAL
50 g butter	2 oz butter
100 g dark soft brown sugar	4 oz dark soft brown sugar
350 g dessert plums	12 oz dessert plums
3 eggs	3 eggs
175 g castor sugar	6 oz castor sugar
175 g self-raising flour	6 oz self-raising flour

Grease a 1-litre/1½-pint pie dish. Melt the butter and brown sugar over a low heat and pour into the dish. Halve the plums and remove the stones. Arrange these cut side down in the butter mixture. Whisk the eggs and sugar together in a bowl over hot water until thick and almost white. Fold in the sifted flour and pour over the plums.

Bake in a moderately hot oven (190°C, 375°F, Gas Mark 5) for 35 minutes. Cool for 5 minutes and turn out on to a warm serving dish. Serve with custard or cream. Serves 4–6

Apple Dumplings with Apricot Sauce

METRIC	IMPERIAL
225 g shortcrust pastry	8 oz shortcrust pastry
4 small cooking apples	4 small cooking apples
25 g raisins	1 oz raisins
25 g light soft brown sugar	1 oz light soft brown sugar
25 g butter	1 oz butter
¼ teaspoon ground cinnamon	¼ teaspoon ground cinnamon
Sauce	*Sauce*
175 g apricot jam	6 oz apricot jam
juice of 1 lemon	juice of 1 lemon
beaten egg to glaze	beaten egg to glaze

Roll out the pastry and cut out four circles the size of a saucer. Peel and core the apples and put one in the centre of each piece of pastry. Mix together the raisins, sugar, butter and cinnamon and use to fill the apples.

Apple Dumplings with Apricot Sauce

Plum Upside-Down Pudding

Enclose the apples in the pastry and arrange on a greased baking tray with the joins underneath. Decorate with pastry leaves. Brush with a little beaten egg and bake in a hot oven (220°C, 425°F, Gas Mark 7) for 25 minutes.

While the apple dumplings are cooking, prepare the sauce. Put the jam and lemon juice in a pan and heat gently until the jam has melted. Put through a sieve and reheat. Serve the dumplings hot with this sauce. They are also very good cold with cream. Serves 4

Marshmallow and Chocolate Fondue

METRIC	IMPERIAL
100 g plain chocolate	4 oz plain chocolate
225 g sugar	8 oz sugar
150 ml strong black coffee	¼ pint strong black coffee
pinch of salt	pinch of salt
6 tablespoons double cream	6 tablespoons double cream
225 g marshmallows	8 oz marshmallows

Grate the chocolate into a bowl and add the sugar, coffee and salt. Rest the bowl over a pan of hot water and heat gently until the chocolate melts. Continue heating and stirring until the sauce is thick and syrupy. Stir in the cream and heat through. Put the bowl on a plate and surround with marshmallows and cocktail sticks so that the sweets may be dipped into the chocolate sauce. If a fondue set is available, the sauce may be kept hot while dipping goes on. Serves 6

Marshmallow and Chocolate Fondue

Iced Walnut Cake

This cake used to be very popular in tearooms, partly because of the unusual frosting which has a texture like soft snow.

METRIC	IMPERIAL
100 g butter	4 oz butter
225 g castor sugar	8 oz castor sugar
2 eggs, separated	2 eggs, separated
175 g plain flour	6 oz plain flour
2 teaspoons baking powder	2 teaspoons baking powder
150 ml milk	$\frac{1}{4}$ pint milk
$\frac{1}{2}$ teaspoon vanilla essence	$\frac{1}{2}$ teaspoon vanilla essence
100 g walnuts, chopped	4 oz walnuts, chopped
Frosting	*Frosting*
1 egg white	1 egg white
175 g castor sugar	6 oz castor sugar
2 tablespoons water	2 tablespoons water
$\frac{1}{4}$ teaspoon cream of tartar	$\frac{1}{4}$ teaspoon cream of tartar
pinch of salt	pinch of salt
walnuts or pecan nuts to decorate	walnuts or pecan nuts to decorate

Cream the butter and sugar and beat in the egg yolks. Sift the flour and baking powder together. Add to the creamed mixture alternately with the milk. Add the vanilla essence and the walnuts. Whisk the egg whites to stiff peaks and fold into the cake. Turn into a greased and base-lined 25-cm/10-inch round cake tin. Bake in a moderate oven (180°C, 350°F, Gas Mark 4) for 1–1$\frac{1}{4}$ hours. Turn out on a wire rack to cool.

Put all the frosting ingredients into a bowl over a pan of fast boiling water. Using a hand whisk, beat the mixture hard until it stands in stiff peaks; this will take about 7 minutes. During cooking, scrape down the sides of the bowl occasionally with a spatula.

Put the cake on to a serving plate. Pour on the frosting and swirl it with the back of a spoon. Decorate with nuts.

Above: Iced Walnut Cake;
below: Devil's Food Cake

Devil's Food Cake

METRIC	IMPERIAL
225 g plain flour	8 oz plain flour
50 g cocoa	2 oz cocoa
1 teaspoon bicarbonate of soda	1 teaspoon bicarbonate of soda
pinch of salt	pinch of salt
275 g castor sugar	10 oz castor sugar
100 g soft margarine	4 oz soft margarine
150 ml sour milk	¼ pint sour milk
2 eggs	2 eggs
Fudge Frosting	*Fudge Frosting*
100 g butter	4 oz butter
175 g light soft brown sugar	6 oz light soft brown sugar
25 g cocoa	1 oz cocoa
5 tablespoons milk	5 tablespoons milk
250 g icing sugar	9 oz icing sugar

Sift the flour, cocoa, bicarbonate of soda and salt into a bowl. Cream the sugar and margarine until light and fluffy. Work in the dry ingredients and the milk alternately, and finally add the eggs. Beat very well until light and soft. Put into two greased and base-lined 20-cm/8-inch sponge tins. Bake in a moderate oven (180°C, 350°F, Gas Mark 4) for 35 minutes. Turn out on to a wire rack to cool.

Put the butter, brown sugar and cocoa into a pan. Bring to the boil and boil for 2 minutes. Stir in the milk and bring back to the boil, stirring well. Sift the icing sugar into a bowl and pour on the cocoa mixture, beating well. Use to fill and top the cake.

Toffee Apples

Hallowe'en Treats

Toffee Apples

METRIC	IMPERIAL
8 small dessert apples	8 small dessert apples
450 g granulated sugar	1 lb granulated sugar
100 g butter	4 oz butter
2 tablespoons water	2 tablespoons water

Remove the stalks of the apples and put a stick well into each apple. Put the sugar, butter and water into a pan and allow the sugar to dissolve slowly over a low heat. Boil the toffee to 140°C/280°F (at this heat a little of the mixture dropped into a cup of cold water will separate into threads which are hard but not brittle). Dip the apples into the toffee until they are well covered, but keep the sticks clean. Rest the sticks in a jam jar until the toffee has just set. Heat the toffee again, and dip the apples a second time. Return to the jar until cold. Eat quickly as they go sticky when kept.

Hallowe'en Punch

Hallowe'en Punch

METRIC	IMPERIAL
8 cloves	8 cloves
1 cinnamon stick, broken	1 cinnamon stick, broken
2 blades mace	2 blades mace
¼ teaspoon grated nutmeg	¼ teaspoon grated nutmeg
1 lemon	1 lemon
1 orange	1 orange
150 ml water	¼ pint water
25 g dark soft brown sugar	1 oz dark soft brown sugar
1·15 litres medium cider	2 pints medium cider

Put the cloves, cinnamon stick, mace and nutmeg in a pan. Peel the lemon and orange thinly and add the peel to the pan with the water and sugar. Bring to the boil slowly and simmer gently for 15 minutes. Strain into a large pan and add the cider. Squeeze the juice from the lemon and orange and add to the pan. Heat until foaming and nearly boiling. Serve hot in pottery mugs or glass tankards with extra fruit if liked. Serves 6

November

The weather
may be gloomy
but the children love
Guy Fawkes' Day (November 5th) with special
cakes and toffee. Those who want a peaceful Christmas
can enjoy making their preparations while
there is plenty of time and dried
fruit is fresh and in
good supply.

Foods in Season

FISH

Carp · Cod · Haddock · Hake · Halibut · Herring · Mackerel · Mussels · Oysters · Pike
Plaice · Scallops · Skate · Sole · Sprats · Whiting

POULTRY AND GAME

Chicken · Duck · Goose · Turkey · Grouse · Hare · Partridge · Pheasant · Rabbit · Snipe
Wild duck · Venison

VEGETABLES
(home produced and imported)

Brussels sprouts · Cabbage · Carrots · Celery · Chicory · Jerusalem artichokes · Leeks
Parsnips · Red cabbage · Spinach · Swedes · Turnips

FRUIT
(home produced and imported)

Apples · Cranberries · Grapes · Lemons · Oranges · Pears · Pomegranates · Tangerines

Freezer Notes

There is little fresh food to be preserved, except for Jerusalem artichokes and root vegetables which are coming into season. It is worth buying Christmas meat and poultry now to be sure to get the weight and type of joint the family requires. This is also a good time to make advance Christmas preparations, and to stock up on cream, ice cream and prepared party dishes.

LTANAS

Soups

Ham and Pea Soup

METRIC	IMPERIAL
450 g dried green peas	1 lb dried green peas
1 large onion, chopped	1 large onion, chopped
1 small turnip, chopped	1 small turnip, chopped
1 large carrot, chopped	1 large carrot, chopped
2·25 litres bacon stock	4 pints bacon stock
pepper	pepper
175 g cooked ham, chopped	6 oz cooked ham, chopped
1 teaspoon chopped mint to garnish	1 teaspoon chopped mint to garnish

Put the peas into a bowl, cover with water and leave to soak for 8 hours. Drain well. Put the peas into a pan with the other vegetables, stock and pepper. Bring to the boil, cover and simmer for 1 hour until the peas are soft. Put through a sieve or purée in a liquidiser. Return to the pan with the chopped ham and reheat. Serve garnished with mint.

This soup can be made with the stock from boiling bacon, and the left-over bacon may be used instead of ham. If the stock is very salty, use half stock and half water. Serves 6

Celery and Cheese Soup

METRIC	IMPERIAL
1 large head celery	1 large head celery
1·15 litres chicken stock	2 pints chicken stock
25 g plain flour	1 oz plain flour
300 ml creamy milk	½ pint creamy milk
salt and pepper	salt and pepper
50 g Cheddar cheese, grated	2 oz Cheddar cheese, grated

Wash the celery very thoroughly and cut into small pieces. Put into a pan with the stock and simmer for 1 hour until the celery is very soft. Put through a sieve or purée in a liquidiser. Mix the flour with a little of the milk to make a smooth paste. Put the celery purée into a pan with the flour paste and the remaining milk. Simmer over a low heat, stirring well for 10 minutes. Season well with salt and pepper. Remove from the heat and stir in the cheese until melted. Serve at once. Serves 4

Left: Ham and Pea Soup; below: Celery and Cheese Soup

Lentil and Smoked Sausage Soup

This soup makes a complete meal as it is very thick and nourishing. Use a smoked pork sausage ring from a delicatessen, or frankfurters if this is not obtainable.

METRIC	IMPERIAL
225 g lentils	8 oz lentils
1 medium onion, chopped	1 medium onion, chopped
50 g bacon, chopped	2 oz bacon, chopped
1·75 litres water	3 pints water
salt and pepper	salt and pepper
225 g smoked sausage	8 oz smoked sausage
150 ml creamy milk	¼ pint creamy milk
pinch of dried sage	pinch of dried sage

Put the lentils into a bowl, cover with cold water, and leave to soak for 8 hours. Drain well. Put the onion and bacon in a pan and heat gently until the fat runs and the onion is soft and golden. Drain off any surplus fat. Add the water and drained lentils to the pan with plenty of salt and pepper. Bring to the boil, then cover and simmer for 1 hour until the lentils are soft. Put through a sieve or purée in a liquidiser. Return to the pan. Cut the sausage into 1-cm/½-inch rings. Add to the soup with the milk and sage. Reheat until piping hot. Serves 4–6

Lentil and Smoked Sausage Soup

Main Dishes

Seafood Spaghetti

METRIC	IMPERIAL
450 g spaghetti	1 lb spaghetti
25 g butter	1 oz butter
300 ml double cream	½ pint double cream
grated rind of 1 lemon	grated rind of 1 lemon
1 tablespoon chopped parsley	1 tablespoon chopped parsley
1 (198-g) can tuna	1 (7-oz) can tuna
100 g peeled prawns	4 oz peeled prawns
salt and pepper	salt and pepper

Heat a large pan of salted water and put in the spaghetti, leaving it long and letting it curl round in the water. Cook for about 12 minutes until just tender. Drain very thoroughly.

While the spaghetti is cooking, prepare the sauce. Melt the butter over very low heat and stir in the cream, lemon rind and parsley. Drain the tuna and cut in chunks. Add the tuna, prawns and seasoning. Heat very gently without boiling. As soon as the spaghetti is cooked, serve on four individual warmed plates and pour on the sauce. Serves 4

Lamb Curry

This is a fairly mild curry which is good served with boiled rice, mango chutney, sliced bananas and desiccated coconut. Curry tastes even better if cooled and stored in the refrigerator overnight, then reheated for serving.

METRIC	IMPERIAL
3 tablespoons oil	3 tablespoons oil
900 g shoulder of lamb, cubed	2 lb shoulder of lamb, cubed
1 clove garlic, crushed	1 clove garlic, crushed
2 large onions, chopped	2 large onions, chopped
1 large cooking apple	1 large cooking apple
2 tablespoons curry powder	2 tablespoons curry powder
1 teaspoon salt	1 teaspoon salt
1 bay leaf	1 bay leaf
grated rind of 1 large lemon	grated rind of 1 large lemon
25 g light soft brown sugar	1 oz light soft brown sugar
25 g sultanas	1 oz sultanas

Heat the oil and brown the lamb cubes on all sides. Add the garlic and onion and stir over low heat for 5 minutes. Peel and core the apple, and cut the flesh into cubes. Add to the pan with the curry powder and continue cooking for 3 minutes. Add the remaining ingredients with 300 ml/½ pint water, cover and simmer for 1½ hours until the liquid is reduced and the lamb is tender. Serve hot with rice and accompaniments. Serves 4–6

Rabbit Pie

METRIC	IMPERIAL
350 g shortcrust pastry	12 oz shortcrust pastry
1 large rabbit, jointed	1 large rabbit, jointed
salt and pepper	salt and pepper
15 g plain flour	½ oz plain flour
1 tablespoon chopped parsley	1 tablespoon chopped parsley
1 small onion, chopped	1 small onion, chopped
350 g bacon, chopped	12 oz bacon, chopped
300 ml chicken stock	½ pint chicken stock

Roll out the pastry to fit a 1·75-litre/3-pint pie dish. Put the joints of rabbit in a bowl and cover with cold salted water. Leave to soak for 1 hour, then drain and dry well. Put the salt, pepper, flour, parsley and onion on to a piece of greaseproof paper and put the rabbit joints on top. Coat the joints in this mixture and put into the pie dish. Sprinkle with the bacon and add the stock. Cover with the pastry lid. Bake in a moderately hot oven (190°C, 375°F, Gas Mark 5) for 1¼ hours. Serve hot or cold. Serves 6

Pork and Potato Bake

METRIC	IMPERIAL
4 rashers streaky bacon, chopped	4 rashers streaky bacon, chopped
1 medium onion, chopped	1 medium onion, chopped
100 g mushrooms, chopped	4 oz mushrooms, chopped
1 teaspoon chopped fresh sage	1 teaspoon chopped fresh sage
salt and pepper	salt and pepper
450 g lean pork, cubed	1 lb lean pork, cubed
450 g potatoes, sliced	1 lb potatoes, sliced
300 ml stock	½ pint stock
25 g dripping	1 oz dripping

Put the bacon into a pan and heat until the fat runs. Add the onion and cook over low heat for 5 minutes. Add the mushrooms and continue cooking for 3 minutes. Stir in the sage and season well. Add the pork and stir gently over a low heat until the pork is just browned. Put a third of this mixture into a deep casserole. Cover with a layer of potatoes, then more pork. Add a second layer of potatoes and the remaining pork. Pour in the stock. Arrange the remaining potatoes on top. Put flakes of dripping on the top of the potatoes. Cover and bake in a moderate oven (180°C, 350°F, Gas Mark 4) for 1¼ hours. Remove the lid and continue cooking for 20 minutes so that the potatoes brown. Serves 4–6

November Treats

Parkin

This dark, solid gingerbread is traditionally eaten in Yorkshire, where Guy Fawkes was born, on November 5th. It is very good eaten with a piece of cheese, and is best stored in a tin for at least a week before using.

METRIC	IMPERIAL
175 g plain flour	6 oz plain flour
1 teaspoon salt	1 teaspoon salt
1 teaspoon ground ginger	1 teaspoon ground ginger
1 teaspoon ground cinnamon	1 teaspoon ground cinnamon
1 teaspoon bicarbonate of soda	1 teaspoon bicarbonate of soda
300 g coarse oatmeal	10 oz coarse oatmeal
175 g black treacle	6 oz black treacle
125 g butter	5 oz butter
100 g dark soft brown sugar	4 oz dark soft brown sugar
150 ml milk	¼ pint milk
1 egg	1 egg

Above right: Bonfire Toffee; above: Parkin

Sift together the flour, salt, ginger, cinnamon and bicarbonate of soda. Stir in the oatmeal. Put the treacle, butter, sugar and milk into a pan and heat gently until the butter has melted. Cool to lukewarm and beat in the egg. Pour into the dry ingredients and beat well until smooth. Put in a greased and lined 18-cm/7-inch square tin. Bake in a moderate oven (180°C, 350°F, Gas Mark 4) for $1\frac{1}{4}$ hours. Leave in the tin for 10 minutes, then turn out on to a wire rack to cool. Keep in an airtight tin for at least a week before cutting.

Bonfire Toffee

Another Yorkshire favourite which is eaten around the bonfire on Guy Fawkes' Night, and which appeals to those with strong teeth.

METRIC	IMPERIAL
450 g granulated sugar	1 lb granulated sugar
50 g butter	2 oz butter
1 tablespoon golden syrup	1 tablespoon golden syrup
1 (227-g) can sweetened condensed milk	1 (8-oz) can sweetened condensed milk
1 teaspoon lemon juice	1 teaspoon lemon juice

Put the sugar, butter and syrup together in a pan and heat gently until they have melted together. Bring to the boil and stir in the condensed milk and lemon juice. Boil hard to 119°C/247°F or when a little of the mixture dropped into a cup of cold water forms a hard ball. Take the pan off the heat and leave to stand until the toffee stops bubbling. Pour into a well-greased tin. Mark into squares when nearly set, but leave until cold and hard before breaking.

Sweet Things

Seed Cake

METRIC	IMPERIAL
450 g plain flour	1 lb plain flour
$\frac{1}{4}$ teaspoon bicarbonate of soda	$\frac{1}{4}$ teaspoon bicarbonate of soda
225 g butter	8 oz butter
200 g castor sugar	7 oz castor sugar
50 g mixed candied peel, chopped	2 oz mixed candied peel, chopped
25 g caraway seeds	1 oz caraway seeds
2 eggs	2 eggs
150 ml milk	$\frac{1}{4}$ pint milk

Sift the flour and bicarbonate of soda together. Rub in the butter and then stir in the sugar. Add the peel and caraway seeds. Beat the eggs and milk together and gradually add to the dry mixture. Beat well to give a soft dropping consistency, adding a little more milk if necessary. Put into a greased 20-cm/8-inch round cake tin. Bake in a moderate oven (180°C, 350°F, Gas Mark 4) for $1\frac{1}{2}$ hours. Cool in the tin for 5 minutes, then turn on to a wire rack to cool.

Date and Walnut Cake

METRIC	IMPERIAL
300 ml milk	$\frac{1}{2}$ pint milk
2 tablespoons golden syrup	2 tablespoons golden syrup
50 g dates, chopped	2 oz dates, chopped
50 g walnuts, chopped	2 oz walnuts, chopped
225 g self-raising flour	8 oz self-raising flour
1 teaspoon bicarbonate of soda	1 teaspoon bicarbonate of soda
pinch of salt	pinch of salt

Put the milk, syrup and dates into a pan and bring to the boil slowly, stirring well. Cool to lukewarm. Add the walnuts, flour, bicarbonate of soda and salt and beat very thoroughly. Put into a greased 0·5-kg/1-lb loaf tin. Bake in a moderate oven (160°C, 325°F, Gas Mark 3) for 45 minutes. Cool on a wire rack. Serve sliced and buttered.

Seed Cake

Date and Walnut Cake

Cherry Almond Cake

METRIC	IMPERIAL
175 g glacé cherries	6 oz glacé cherries
200 g self-raising flour	7 oz self-raising flour
pinch of salt	pinch of salt
100 g butter	4 oz butter
100 g castor sugar	4 oz castor sugar
3 eggs	3 eggs
25 g ground almonds	1 oz ground almonds

Wash and dry the cherries and cut them into quarters. Sift the flour and salt. Sprinkle the cherries with a little of the flour so that they are lightly coated. Cream the butter until soft and then beat in the sugar until light and fluffy. Beat in the eggs one at a time with a little of the flour. Stir in the remaining flour, almonds and cherries. Put into a greased and lined 15-cm/6-inch round cake tin. Bake in a moderate oven (180°C, 350°F, Gas Mark 4) for 1 hour 20 minutes. Cool on a wire rack.

Cherry Almond Cake

Preparing for the Festive Season

Black Bun

This is rather like a rich fruit cake inside a pastry case, and is a traditional dish for New Year's Eve in Scotland. It is best made a few weeks before it is needed, and stored in a tin.

METRIC	IMPERIAL
350 g shortcrust pastry	12 oz shortcrust pastry
225 g plain flour	8 oz plain flour
100 g granulated sugar	4 oz granulated sugar
450 g raisins, stoned	1 lb raisins, stoned
450 g currants	1 lb currants
100 g mixed candied peel, chopped	4 oz mixed candied peel, chopped
100 g almonds, chopped	4 oz almonds, chopped
1 teaspoon ground coriander	1 teaspoon ground coriander
1 teaspoon caraway seeds	1 teaspoon caraway seeds
1 teaspoon ground ginger	1 teaspoon ground ginger
1 teaspoon ground cinnamon	1 teaspoon ground cinnamon
1 teaspoon ground allspice	1 teaspoon ground allspice
¼ teaspoon black pepper	¼ teaspoon black pepper
½ teaspoon cream of tartar	½ teaspoon cream of tartar
¼ teaspoon bicarbonate of soda	¼ teaspoon bicarbonate of soda
6 tablespoons milk	6 tablespoons milk
beaten egg to glaze	beaten egg to glaze

1 · Roll out the pastry and use three-quarters of it to line a deep 20-cm/8-inch round cake tin.

Mix all the other ingredients together using the hands.

2 · Press the filling into the pastry case. Level the top.

Roll out the remaining pastry to make a lid and put on top of the filling.

3 · Pinch the edges together and prick the lid a few times with a fork.

Brush well with beaten egg. Bake in a cool oven (150°C, 300°F, Gas Mark 2) for 3½ hours. Leave in the tin for 10 minutes, then turn out carefully and cool on a wire rack. When cold, store in a tin for 4 to 6 weeks before cutting.

Black Bun

Christmas Cake

Christmas Cake

This rich moist cake will keep in a tin for at least eight months, and it is a good filling cake for a lunch box or picnic hamper. When finished with almond paste and royal icing, it makes a tempting Christmas cake which will not linger, and is just as good for a wedding or christening celebration.

METRIC	IMPERIAL
225 g butter	8 oz butter
225 g light soft brown sugar	8 oz light soft brown sugar
1 tablespoon black treacle	1 tablespoon black treacle
4 eggs	4 eggs
4 tablespoons cold tea without milk	4 tablespoons cold tea without milk
grated rind of 1 lemon	grated rind of 1 lemon
½ teaspoon vanilla essence	½ teaspoon vanilla essence
100 g self-raising flour	4 oz self-raising flour
175 g plain flour	6 oz plain flour
1 teaspoon ground mixed spice	1 teaspoon ground mixed spice
¼ teaspoon salt	¼ teaspoon salt
350 g currants	12 oz currants
350 g sultanas	12 oz sultanas
225 g raisins, stoned	8 oz raisins, stoned
50 g mixed candied peel, chopped	2 oz mixed candied peel, chopped
50 g glacé cherries, halved	2 oz glacé cherries, halved
almond paste	almond paste
royal icing	royal icing

Cream the butter and sugar until light and fluffy. Put the treacle, eggs, tea, lemon rind and vanilla in a bowl and break up just enough for the eggs to be lightly mixed. Sift the flours, spice and salt into a large mixing bowl. Add the liquid and flour mixtures alternately to the creamed fat. Mix well but do not beat. Add the currants, sultanas, raisins, peel and cherries and mix just enough to distribute evenly. The mixture should be just stiff enough to fall easily from a spoon.

Grease and line a 25-cm/10-inch round cake tin. Spoon in the mixture and level off with a spoon. Leave to stand for 1 hour. Bake in a cool oven (150°C, 300°F, Gas Mark 2) for 4 hours. If the top of the cake becomes very brown, cover it with a piece of greaseproof paper halfway through cooking. Leave the cake in the tin until just warm, then turn out on a wire rack to finish cooling. Store in a tin until needed. Coat with almond paste 3 days before finally finishing the cake with royal icing.

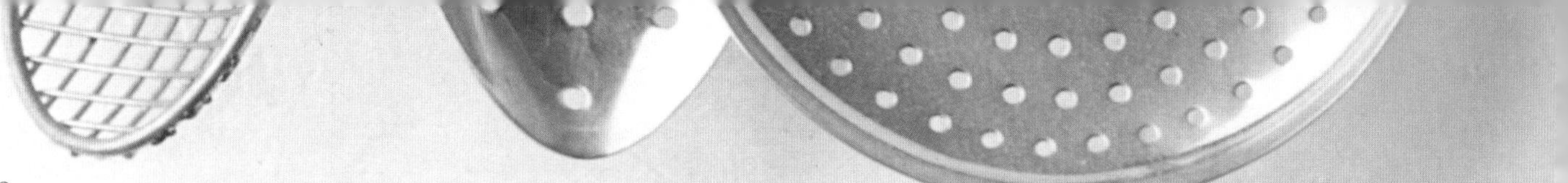

Christmas Pudding

This recipe makes a light and delicious pudding. Unused puddings may be stored in a cool dry place, or in the freezer.

METRIC	IMPERIAL
225 g self-raising flour	8 oz self-raising flour
225 g fresh white breadcrumbs	8 oz fresh white breadcrumbs
225 g shredded suet	8 oz shredded suet
225 g currants	8 oz currants
350 g sultanas	12 oz sultanas
350 g raisins, stoned	12 oz raisins, stoned
225 g dark soft brown sugar	8 oz dark soft brown sugar
6 eggs	6 eggs
grated rind and juice of 1 orange	grated rind and juice of 1 orange
grated rind and juice of 1 lemon	grated rind and juice of 1 lemon
1 teaspoon salt	1 teaspoon salt
1 teaspoon ground mixed spice	1 teaspoon ground mixed spice
300 ml brown ale	½ pint brown ale
100 g mixed candied peel, chopped	4 oz mixed candied peel, chopped
100 g glacé cherries, chopped	4 oz glacé cherries, chopped
1 small apple, grated	1 small apple, grated
1 small carrot, grated	1 small carrot, grated

Put the flour, breadcrumbs, suet, currants, sultanas, raisins and sugar into a large mixing bowl. Break in the eggs. Add the orange and lemon rind and juice to the fruit mixture with the salt, spice, ale, peel, cherries, apple and carrot. Mix very thoroughly with a wooden spoon. The mixture will be stiff, but not dry. Put into four greased 1-litre/1½-pint pudding basins. Cover each with a piece of greaseproof paper and then with kitchen foil. Tie securely with string. Put into a pan of boiling water to come halfway up the basins. Cover and boil for 8 hours, topping up with boiling water from time to time. Remove from the pan and replace the old covers with clean paper. Store in a cool, dry place, or wrap and freeze. When needed, boil for 3 hours before serving. Serve with cream, hard sauce or custard. Each pudding serves 8

Below: Christmas Pudding; right: Cider Mincemeat

Cider Mincemeat

METRIC	IMPERIAL
350 g cooking apples	12 oz cooking apples
350 g raisins	12 oz raisins
175 g currants	6 oz currants
175 g light soft brown sugar	6 oz light soft brown sugar
2 teaspoons ground cinnamon	2 teaspoons ground cinnamon
1 teaspoon ground cloves	1 teaspoon ground cloves
1 teaspoon grated nutmeg	1 teaspoon grated nutmeg
4½ tablespoons dry cider	4½ tablespoons dry cider
grated rind and juice of 1 lemon	grated rind and juice of 1 lemon
75 g butter	3 oz butter
1 tablespoon brandy	1 tablespoon brandy

Peel and core the apples. Chop the apples and the raisins finely. Put into a pan with the sugar, cinnamon, cloves, nutmeg and cider. Add the lemon juice and rind to the pan. Add the butter. Simmer for 30 minutes, stirring well. Cool and stir in the brandy. Leave until cold before putting into sterilised jars and covering.

Note This makes a small quantity (1 kg/2 lb) of mincemeat which is enough for most families. It will keep in a refrigerator for 4 weeks.

December

It is difficult to think about anything except Christmas meals now, but many preparations can be made with the aid of the freezer. The conventional meals can be varied with some of the old-fashioned recipes which our ancestors used to enjoy.

Foods in Season

FISH

Carp · Cod · Haddock · Hake · Halibut · Herring · Mussels · Oysters · Pike · Plaice
Scallops · Skate · Sole · Sprats · Whiting

POULTRY AND GAME

Chicken · Duck · Goose · Turkey · Grouse · Hare · Partridge · Pheasant · Rabbit · Snipe
Wild duck · Venison

VEGETABLES
(home produced and imported)

Brussels sprouts · Cabbage · Carrots · Celery · Chicory · Jerusalem artichokes · Leeks
Parsnips · Red cabbage · Spinach · Swedes · Turnips

FRUIT
(home produced and imported)

Apples · Cranberries · Grapes · Lemons · Oranges · Pears · Pomegranates · Tangerines

Freezer Notes

Cranberries and tangerines are worth freezing as they have such a short season. Stuffings and sauces may be made and frozen at the beginning of the month to avoid a rush on Christmas Day, and party cakes and puddings may also be prepared in advance. After Christmas, use the freezer to preserve poultry stocks and soups, leftover meat or poultry, and surplus supplies of dried fruit and candied fruit which keep well and remain fresh-tasting.

NAPOLÉON

Soups and Starters

Chestnut Cream Soup

METRIC	IMPERIAL
450 g chestnuts	1 lb chestnuts
1 large onion, sliced	1 large onion, sliced
40 g butter	$1\frac{1}{2}$ oz butter
1 medium potato, chopped	1 medium potato, chopped
3 sticks celery, chopped	3 sticks celery, chopped
1·4 litres beef stock	$2\frac{1}{2}$ pints beef stock
salt and pepper	salt and pepper
$\frac{1}{2}$ teaspoon light soft brown sugar	$\frac{1}{2}$ teaspoon light soft brown sugar
pinch of dried mixed herbs	pinch of dried mixed herbs
15 g plain flour	$\frac{1}{2}$ oz plain flour
300 ml milk	$\frac{1}{2}$ pint milk
1 tablespoon dry sherry	1 tablespoon dry sherry

Make a short cut in the hard shell of each chestnut. Put the chestnuts into a pan of boiling water and simmer for 20 minutes. Remove the hard shells and rub off the brown skins. Chop the chestnuts roughly. Put the onion into a pan with half the butter and cook gently until soft. Add the potato, celery, chestnuts, stock, salt and pepper. Bring to the boil, then cover and simmer until the chestnuts are soft. Press through a sieve, or purée in a liquidiser.

Melt the remaining butter and work in the flour. Cook for 2 minutes and add the sugar and herbs. Stir in the chestnut purée. Reheat gently until heated through. Add the milk and reheat to almost boiling point. Stir in the sherry and serve at once. Serves 4–6

Hot Mackerel Pots

Smoked mackerel is easily obtained from fishmongers or freezer cabinets.

METRIC	IMPERIAL
4 fillets smoked mackerel	4 fillets smoked mackerel
300 ml cheese sauce	$\frac{1}{2}$ pint cheese sauce
pinch of dry mustard	pinch of dry mustard
25 g fresh white breadcrumbs	1 oz fresh white breadcrumbs
25 g Cheddar cheese, grated	1 oz Cheddar cheese, grated

Skin the mackerel fillets and flake the fish into large pieces. Fold them into the cheese sauce carefully so that the pieces are not broken too small. Add the mustard. Grease four individual ramekins and put in the fish mixture. Mix the breadcrumbs and cheese and sprinkle on top of the mackerel. Bake in a moderate oven (180°C, 350°F, Gas Mark 4) for 20 minutes. Serve very hot. Serves 4

Chestnut Cream Soup; Hot Mackerel Pots

Citrus Starter

METRIC	IMPERIAL
2 grapefruit	2 grapefruit
1 orange	1 orange
225 g peeled shrimps	8 oz peeled shrimps
5 tablespoons mayonnaise	5 tablespoons mayonnaise
1 teaspoon chopped mint to garnish	1 teaspoon chopped mint to garnish

Peel the grapefruit and orange. Remove all the white pith and divide the fruit into segments. Skin the segments carefully so that the pieces of fruit remain whole. Put the fruit into a bowl and add the shrimps. Stir in the mayonnaise to coat the fruit and shrimps. Spoon the mixture into glasses and sprinkle with mint. Serves 4–6

Christmas Feast

Roast Turkey with Sausage Stuffing

METRIC	IMPERIAL
1 (4·5-kg) turkey	1 (10-lb) turkey
450 g pork sausagemeat	1 lb pork sausagemeat
50 g streaky bacon, chopped	2 oz streaky bacon, chopped
liver of the turkey	liver of the turkey
1 medium onion, chopped	1 medium onion, chopped
15 g butter	½ oz butter
1 egg	1 egg
50 g fresh white breadcrumbs	2 oz fresh white breadcrumbs
salt and pepper	salt and pepper
2 teaspoons dried mixed herbs	2 teaspoons dried mixed herbs
225 g butter	8 oz butter

Put a large sheet of kitchen foil into a roasting tin and place the turkey on it. Put the sausagemeat in a bowl and add the bacon. Cut the liver into small pieces and put into a pan with the onion and butter. Cook and stir over low heat until soft. Mix with the sausagemeat, beaten egg, breadcrumbs, salt, pepper and herbs. Mix well but do not add any extra moistening, as the stuffing absorbs meat juices during the cooking.

Put the stuffing into the body cavity of the turkey. Spread the butter all over the breast of the bird and fold the foil over lightly to cover it. Put into a hot oven (220°C, 425°F, Gas Mark 7) for 30 minutes, then reduce the heat to moderately hot (190°C, 375°F, Gas Mark 5) and cook for 2½ hours. Open the foil for the last 30 minutes to brown the skin. Leave to stand for 20 minutes so that the flesh is firm enough to carve well. Serves 10–12

Roast Turkey with Sausage Stuffing

Sprouts with Almonds and Mushrooms

Parsnip Purée

Sprouts with Almonds and Mushrooms

METRIC	IMPERIAL
675 g Brussels sprouts	1½ lb Brussels sprouts
225 g button mushrooms	8 oz button mushrooms
75 g butter	3 oz butter
50 g blanched almonds	2 oz blanched almonds
salt and pepper	salt and pepper

Remove any discoloured leaves from the sprouts and cut a tiny cross in their stems. Put into a pan of boiling salted water and boil until the sprouts are just tender but still firm so that they keep a slightly crisp texture. Drain very thoroughly.

While the sprouts are cooking, wipe the mushrooms. Melt 50 g/2 oz of the butter and toss the mushrooms over a low heat until just cooked. In a separate pan, melt the remaining butter and toss the almonds until golden.

Put the drained sprouts into a serving dish and season with salt and pepper. Add the mushrooms and their cooking juices and toss well to mix the sprouts and mushrooms. Sprinkle with the golden almonds and serve at once. Serves 4 – 6

Parsnip Purée

METRIC	IMPERIAL
675 g parsnips	1½ lb parsnips
75 g butter	3 oz butter
150 ml milk	¼ pint milk
salt and pepper	salt and pepper
pinch of grated nutmeg	pinch of grated nutmeg

Peel the parsnips. Cut them in quarters and cut out any hard central core. Cut into small pieces and put into a pan. Cover with cold salted water and boil until the parsnips are tender but not broken. Drain very thoroughly. Put the butter and milk into a small pan and bring to the boil. Pour on to the parsnips and beat until soft. Season well with salt, pepper and nutmeg. Beat until very soft and creamy. Reheat gently and serve hot. Serves 4 – 6

Leg of Pork
with Onion Stuffing
served with Stuffed Cranberry Apples

Leg of Pork with Onion Stuffing

A joint of pork with crisp crackling makes a good alternative to poultry for a festive meal. In country families, pork used to be served to accompany a chicken or turkey, and the two meats make a pleasant contrast.

METRIC	IMPERIAL
1 (2·25-kg) leg of pork, boned	1 (5-lb) leg of pork, boned
2 large onions, chopped	2 large onions, chopped
2 tablespoons chopped fresh sage	2 tablespoons chopped fresh sage
2 tablespoons oil	2 tablespoons oil
salt and pepper	salt and pepper
50 g fresh white breadcrumbs	2 oz fresh white breadcrumbs

Ask the butcher to score the pork skin at 1-cm/$\frac{1}{2}$-inch intervals. Put the onions and sage into a pan with half the oil and cook over a low heat, stirring well, until the onions are soft but not coloured. Season well with salt and pepper and mix with the breadcrumbs.

Insert this stuffing into the bone cavity of the meat and tie the joint very firmly. Put into a roasting tin and brush the remaining oil over the crackling. Sprinkle the oiled surface with salt. Put into a hot oven (220°C, 425°F, Gas Mark 7) for 20 minutes. Reduce the heat to moderate (180°C, 350°F, Gas Mark 4) and continue cooking for 2 hours. Serve hot with gravy and chosen vegetables. Serves 8

Stuffed Cranberry Apples

This colourful combination of cranberries and apples has a deliciously refreshing flavour, and the apples make a good accompaniment to turkey or pork.

METRIC	IMPERIAL
8 dessert apples	8 dessert apples
225 g cranberries	8 oz cranberries
50 g sugar	2 oz sugar
4 tablespoons water	4 tablespoons water
25 g butter	1 oz butter

Wipe the apples but do not peel them. Core the apples and score the skin halfway down, going right round the fruit. Arrange in a greased ovenproof dish. Fill the apples with cranberries and sugar. Pour on the water. Cut the butter into small flakes and put on top of the apples. Bake in a moderate oven (180°C, 350°F, Gas Mark 4) for 30 minutes. Baste with the juices and continue cooking for 10 minutes. Serve from the dish, or arrange round the roast turkey or pork. Serves 8

Stilton Flan

There is often a piece of Stilton cheese left after the Christmas meals, and it gives a splendid flavour to a savoury flan. If Stilton is not available, any blue cheese may be used.

METRIC	IMPERIAL
225 g shortcrust pastry	8 oz shortcrust pastry
75 g butter	3 oz butter
225 g onions, sliced	8 oz onions, sliced
salt and pepper	salt and pepper
25 g plain flour	1 oz plain flour
300 ml milk	½ pint milk
pinch of dry mustard	pinch of dry mustard
100 g Stilton cheese, crumbled	4 oz Stilton cheese, crumbled

Roll out the pastry to line a 20-cm/8-inch flan ring. Roll out the trimmings and cut them into 1-cm/½-inch strips to use as a lattice topping. Melt 50 g/2 oz of the butter and cook the onions until soft and golden. Season and then add the remaining butter. Mix in the flour, work in well and gradually add the milk. Cook and stir over a low heat until the sauce is creamy. Remove from the heat, stir in the mustard and cheese.

Put into the pastry case and cover with a lattice of pastry strips. Bake in a hot oven (220°C, 425°F, Gas Mark 7) for 15 minutes. Reduce the heat to moderate (180°C, 350°F, Gas Mark 4) for 20 minutes. Serve hot. Serves 6–8

Turkey and Ham Pie

METRIC	IMPERIAL
350 g frozen puff pastry	12 oz frozen puff pastry
350 g cooked turkey, chopped	12 oz cooked turkey, chopped
225 g cooked ham, chopped	8 oz cooked ham, chopped
2 eggs, hard-boiled and quartered	2 eggs, hard-boiled and quartered
25 g butter	1 oz butter
25 g plain flour	1 oz plain flour
150 ml milk	¼ pint milk
150 ml turkey stock	¼ pint turkey stock
grated rind and juice of ½ lemon	grated rind and juice of ½ lemon
1 tablespoon chopped parsley	1 tablespoon chopped parsley
beaten egg to glaze	beaten egg to glaze

Roll out the pastry to cover a 1-litre/1½-pint pie dish. Put the turkey and ham into the dish, and arrange the eggs on top. Melt the butter and stir in the flour. Cook for 1 minute and then add the milk and turkey stock gradually. Stir over a low heat until the sauce is thick and creamy. Remove from the heat. Stir in the lemon rind and juice and the parsley, season to taste and pour over the turkey. Cover with the pastry and brush with the beaten egg. Make a hole in the centre of the lid. Bake in a hot oven (220°C, 425°F, Gas Mark 7) for 30 minutes. Serves 4

Below left: Stilton Flan; below right: Turkey and Ham pie

Sweet Things

Old English Trifle

METRIC	IMPERIAL
8 trifle sponge cakes	8 trifle sponge cakes
100 g raspberry jam	4 oz raspberry jam
150 ml sweet sherry	¼ pint sweet sherry
600 ml egg custard	1 pint egg custard
100 g ratafia biscuits	4 oz ratafia biscuits
2 tablespoons brandy	2 tablespoons brandy
450 ml double cream	¾ pint double cream
2 teaspoons castor sugar	2 teaspoons castor sugar
50 g blanched almonds	2 oz blanched almonds
50 g maraschino cherries	2 oz maraschino cherries

Split the sponges in half and then sandwich them together again with the jam. Arrange in a large serving bowl, and sprinkle on the sherry. Leave to stand for 2 hours. Make the custard, cool slightly and pour over the sponge cakes. Leave until cold.

Sprinkle the ratafia biscuits with brandy and put two-thirds of them in a layer over the custard. Put the cream and sugar in a bowl and whip the cream until it stands in soft peaks. Spoon over the custard. Decorate with blanched almonds, cherries and the remaining ratafia biscuits. Serves 6

Syllabub

METRIC	IMPERIAL
150 ml sweet white wine	¼ pint sweet white wine
1 lemon	1 lemon
1 tablespoon dry sherry	1 tablespoon dry sherry
2 tablespoons brandy	2 tablespoons brandy
50 g castor sugar	2 oz castor sugar
300 ml double cream	½ pint double cream

Put the wine into a large bowl. Peel the lemon thinly and put the peel into the wine. Squeeze out the lemon juice and strain it into the wine. Add the sherry and brandy. Leave to stand for 8 hours. Take out the lemon peel and discard. Stir the sugar into the wine and pour in the cream. Whip the mixture until it forms soft peaks. This will take at least 5 minutes, and the mixture will splash a lot until it thickens, so the bowl must be large. Spoon the soft mixture into four or six large wine glasses. Chill before serving with small sweet biscuits. Serves 4–6

Old English Trifle

Pineapple with Brandy Fruit Salad

METRIC	IMPERIAL
1 large pineapple	1 large pineapple
4 tangerines	4 tangerines
100 g sultanas	4 oz sultanas
75 g castor sugar	3 oz castor sugar
pinch of ground ginger	pinch of ground ginger
150 ml brandy	¼ pint brandy
8 scoops lemon sorbet	8 scoops lemon sorbet

Keep the crown of leaves on the pineapple, and split the fruit in half, through the leaves, to form two neat halves. Using a sharp knife, cut the flesh from the pineapple skins, leaving a shell about 2·5 cm/1 inch wide. Put the flesh into a bowl with any juice which runs, and chop into small neat pieces.

Peel the tangerines and divide them into segments. Skin the segments and put them into the bowl. Add the sultanas, sugar, ginger, and brandy and stir well. Leave to stand for 4 hours, stirring often, so that the sugar dissolves and forms a syrup. Just before serving, put the pineapple shells on a large serving plate. Fill with the fruit mixture and syrup. Top with scoops of lemon sorbet and serve at once. Serves 8

Syllabub

Pineapple with Brandy Fruit Salad

Front: Chocolate and Chestnut Log; back right: Star Mince Pies

Star Mince Pies

METRIC	IMPERIAL
350 g shortcrust pastry	12 oz shortcrust pastry
450 g mincemeat	1 lb mincemeat
icing sugar to dust	icing sugar to dust

Roll out the pastry and cut off a third for the lids. Cut the rest to line tartlet tins. Put 2 generous teaspoons mincemeat into each pastry case. Roll out the remaining pastry and cut with a star-shaped biscuit cutter. Arrange on top of the mincemeat so that the tips of the star just meet the pastry case. Bake in a moderately hot oven (190°C, 375°F, Gas Mark 5) for 25 minutes until the pastry is crisp and golden. Cool on a wire rack. Just before serving, sprinkle the star lids thickly with sifted icing sugar. Makes 20

Hard Sauce

This sauce is traditionally served with mince pies and Christmas pudding. It may be made in advance and stored in the refrigerator or freezer.

METRIC	IMPERIAL
100 g butter	4 oz butter
175 g castor sugar	6 oz castor sugar
pinch of grated nutmeg	pinch of grated nutmeg
2 tablespoons brandy	2 tablespoons brandy

Cream the butter until soft and gradually beat in the castor sugar until the mixture is creamy. Add the nutmeg and then the brandy, drop by drop, until it is absorbed, beating all the time. Put into a serving dish and chill until firm.

Chocolate and Chestnut Log

A chocolate log cake is traditionally for the family, but this version is more suitable for a buffet party. For ease of preparation, use a can or tube of sweetened chestnut purée.

METRIC	IMPERIAL
3 eggs	3 eggs
100 g castor sugar	4 oz castor sugar
3 drops of vanilla essence	3 drops of vanilla essence
75 g self-raising flour	3 oz self-raising flour
15 g cocoa	½ oz cocoa
25 g butter, melted	1 oz butter, melted
1 tablespoon hot water	1 tablespoon hot water
castor sugar to sprinkle	castor sugar to sprinkle
225 g sweetened chestnut purée	8 oz sweetened chestnut purée
50 g plain chocolate	2 oz plain chocolate
150 ml double cream	¼ pint double cream
6 marrons glacés	6 marrons glacés

Line an 18 × 28-cm/7 × 11-inch tin with greased greaseproof paper. Whisk the eggs, sugar and vanilla until pale and thick. Sift together the flour and cocoa and fold into the whisked mixture. Fold in the melted butter and water and spread in the prepared tin. Bake in a hot oven (220°C, 425°F, Gas Mark 7) for 10 minutes.

Put a piece of greaseproof paper on a table, and sprinkle it with a little castor sugar. Turn the cake on to this and quickly trim off the edges of the cake with a sharp knife. Roll up the paper and cake together firmly but lightly. Leave until almost cold.

Put the chestnut purée into a bowl. Melt the chocolate over hot water and fold into the purée. Whip the cream to soft peaks and blend into the purée until the mixture is evenly coloured. Unroll the cake carefully and spread it with a third of the cream mixture. Roll up gently and put on to a serving plate. Put the remaining cream all over the cake and mark it lightly with a fork to look like a log. Put the marrons glacés in a line on top of the cake. Chill for 1 hour before serving. Serves 8

Yule Loaf

This used to be made in farmhouses before the development of the iced Christmas cake eaten today. It is best made two or three weeks before use so that the flavour matures. It is usually served sliced and buttered.

METRIC	IMPERIAL
100 g butter	4 oz butter
175 g sugar	6 oz sugar
1 egg	1 egg
100 g raisins, stoned	4 oz raisins, stoned
100 g sultanas	4 oz sultanas
100 g currants	4 oz currants
25 g almonds, chopped	1 oz almonds, chopped
50 g mixed candied peel, chopped	2 oz mixed candied peel, chopped
350 g plain flour	12 oz plain flour
½ teaspoon baking powder	½ teaspoon baking powder
¼ teaspoon bicarbonate of soda	¼ teaspoon bicarbonate of soda
5 tablespoons milk	5 tablespoons milk
pinch of ground mace	pinch of ground mace
3 tablespoons dark rum	3 tablespoons dark rum

Beat the butter, sugar and egg together until creamy. Add the raisins, sultanas, currants and nuts. Sift the flour and baking powder together. Stir the bicarbonate of soda into the milk. Add the flour and milk alternately to the creamed mixture. Add the mace and rum and beat well. Put into a greased and base-lined 1-kg/2-lb loaf tin. Bake in a moderate oven (180°C, 350°F, Gas Mark 4) for 2¼ hours. Cool on a wire rack and store in a tin.

Party Fare

Party Kebabs

METRIC	IMPERIAL
450 g bottled mussels	1 lb bottled mussels
225 g streaky bacon rashers	8 oz streaky bacon rashers
tartare sauce to serve	tartare sauce to serve

Drain the mussels in a colander and rinse them well under cold water. Dry on absorbent paper. Remove the rind from the bacon rashers. Cut each piece of bacon into three pieces and flatten each piece with a wide-bladed knife until the bacon is very thin. Roll a piece of bacon round each mussel.

Remove the rack from the grill pan, and put in the wrapped mussels. Grill under medium heat, turning once, until the bacon becomes crisp. Put a bowl of tartare sauce in the middle of a serving dish. Spear two bacon-wrapped mussels on each cocktail stick, and arrange round the bowl of sauce. Serve very hot.

Cheese Party Puffs

METRIC	IMPERIAL
1 egg	1 egg
100 g Cheddar cheese, finely grated	4 oz Cheddar cheese, finely grated
½ teaspoon salt	½ teaspoon salt
pinch of cayenne pepper	pinch of cayenne pepper
oil to deep fry	oil to deep fry

Separate the egg and put the yolk into a bowl with the cheese, salt and cayenne. Whisk the egg whites to stiff peaks. Fold into the cheese mixture, making sure the cheese is well mixed. Drop spoonfuls of the mixture into hot oil and cook for about 3 minutes until the puffs are golden brown. Drain on absorbent paper and serve very hot. Serves 4

Party Kebabs

Cheese Party Puffs

Christmas Rum Punch

Christmas Rum Punch

The proportions of this punch may be reduced to serve just one or two people. Serve the punch in thick glasses or pottery mugs.

METRIC	IMPERIAL
600 ml dark rum	1 pint dark rum
300 ml brandy	
4 lemons	4 lemons
1·15 litres boiling water	2 pints boiling water
50 g sugar	2 oz sugar
½ teaspoon grated nutmeg	½ teaspoon grated nutmeg

Put the rum and brandy into a large pan. Do not peel the lemons but cut them across in thin slices. Add to the pan with the boiling water, sugar and nutmeg. Heat just to boiling point and pour into mugs. Serves 8–10

Index